MacBo

With m1 chip

User Guide

The Ultimate step by step manual To
Master The MacBook Pro 2020 Version
For Beginners and newbies and Seniors.

By

Emil Adah

Table of Contents

INTRODUCTION

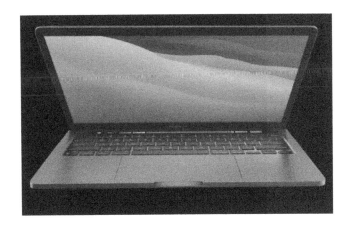

The MacBook Pro models are Apple's most powerful mobile computers. The 13 "model has also been available with the Apple M1 chip as an alternative to the Intel Core i5 and i7 chips since autumn 2020. The Touch Bar with Touch ID sensor (in all current models) automatically adapts to the tasks that you are currently working on.

The models with Apple M1 and Intel 1.4 GHz chip have two Thunderbolt 3 ports - all other variants have four. At 1.37 kg , the 13 "models with Retina display are only slightly heavier than a MacBook Air. The 16" models (from 2019) weigh 2.00 kg. According to Apple, the battery lasts up to 20 hours (13 ") or 11 hours (16").

CHAPTER ONE

SET UP MACBOOK PRO

When you start your MacBook Pro for the first time, the Setup Assistant will guide you through the simple steps required to start using a brand new Mac.

TIP: Press the Escape key to hear how to use "Narration" to set up your Mac. Press Command + Option + F5 to view auxiliary usage options.

Choose a country or region to set the language and time zone of your Mac. You can respond to all prompts, or skip some prompts and select it when you see the "Set Up Later" option. For example, after the first setup, you can still set up Apple Pay (a verified credit card) and "screen time" (you can set it for different users).

Connect to a Wi-Fi network: select the network and enter the password as required. (If you use an Ethernet network, you can also choose "Other network options".) To change the network later, click the menu bar or the Wi-Fi status 📶 icon in the "Control Center", and click "Other network", then select the Wi-Fi network and enter the password. You may choose to activate or deactivate Wi-Fi here.

> **TIP** After setting, if you do not see the Wi-Fi status image 📶 in the menu bar, you can add it. Open "System Preferences" and click "Network". Click Wi-Fi in the list on the left, and then select "Show Wi-Fi status in the menu bar".

- Transfer information: If you plan to set up a new computer and have not set up your Mac before, click "Don't send any information now."

- Login with Apple ID: Your Apple ID is composed of email address and password. Apple ID is the account you use to use all Apple services, including use of App Store, Apple TV App, Apple Bookstore, iCloud, "Messages", etc. Log in with the same Apple ID , and you can use any Apple service on any device, whether it is your computer, iOS device, iPadOS device or Apple Watch. It is recommended that you have your own Apple ID and do not share it with others. If you do not have an Apple ID, you can create a free account during the setup period.

- Screen usage time: Monitor and obtain reports on computer usage.

- Enable Siri and "Hey Siri": You can turn on Siri and "Hey Siri" during the setting. To enable "Hey Siri", say a few Siri commands when prompted.

- Store files in iCloud: Using iCloud services, you can store all content in the cloud, such as documents, videos, music, photos, etc., and access these content from any location. Please make sure that the same Apple ID is logged on each device. To set this option later, please open "System Preferences" and log in with your Apple ID (if you are not already logged in). Click Apple ID, click iCloud in the sidebar, and select the function you want to use.

- Choose Appearance: Select "Light", "Dark" or "Auto" for the desktop appearance. If you want to change the options you selected during setup, please open "System Preferences", click "General", and select an appearance option. other preferences can be set here.

- Set Touch ID: You can add fingerprints to Touch ID during setting. To set up Touch ID later or add another fingerprint, please open "System Preferences" and click Touch ID. To add a fingerprint, click $+$ and follow the screen instructions.

You can also set options for how to use Touch ID on your MacBook Pro: unlock your Mac, use Apple Pay , purchase in the App Store, Apple TV App, Apple "Bookstore" and website Project, and automatically fill in the password.

ATTENTION: If there are two or more users using the same MacBook Pro, each individual user can add fingerprints to Touch ID to authenticate, quickly unlock, and sign in to MacBook Pro. up to 3 fingerprints for each user account can be added, and up to 5 fingerprints in total can be added by all MacBook Pro users.

- Set up Apple Pay: During the MacBook Pro setup, you can set up Apple Pay for a user account. Other users can still use Apple Pay to pay, but they must use an iPhone or Apple Watch with Apple Pay to complete the purchase follow the prompts on the screen to add and verify the card. If you have already used a card when purchasing media, you may be prompted to verify the card first.

To set up Apple Pay or add other cards later, please open "System Preferences" and click "Wallet and Apple Pay". Follow the on-screen instructions to set up Apple Pay.

ATTENTION: The card issuer decides whether your card is eligible for Apple Pay, and may need you to giveextra information to finalize the verification process. Apple Pay can be used with a host of credit and debit cards.

BACKUP AND RESTORE YOUR MAC

In order to keep your files safe and secure, please back up your MacBook Pro regularly. The easiest way to back up is to use the built-in function of Mac "Time Machine" to back up apps, accounts, preferences, music, photos, videos and files (the macOS operating system is not backed up). Use "Time Machine" to back up to an external storage device connected to MacBook Pro or a supported network file.

ATTENTION: You can use a shared Mac connected to the same network as the MacBook

Pro as the backup destination. On another Mac, go to the "Sharing" panel in "System Preferences" and turn on "File Sharing". To add a shared folder, hold down the Control key and click the folder, select "Advanced Options", and then click "Share as Time Machine Target".

Set "Time Machine". Ensure to connect your MacBook Pro to the same Wi-Fi network as the external storage device, or better still connect the external storage device to the MacBook pro. Touch "System Preferences", tap "Time Machine", and choose "Auto Backup". Choose the drive you want to use for the backup, and you're done.

Use iCloud backup. Files in "iCloud Drive" and photos in "iCloud Photos" are automatically stored in iCloud, so there is no need to back up through "Time Machine". However, if you want to back up these items, do the following:

- o iCloud Dri**ve:** select "System Preferences", touch Apple ID, then tap on iCloud and deselect "Optimize Mac Storage". The contents of "iCloud Drive" will be stored on your Mac and included in the backup.

10

o iCloud Photos: select "Photos", then select "Photos"> "Preferences...". Touch "Download original file to this Mac" in the iCloud panel. The entire resolution version of the whole photo library will be cataloged on the Mac and incorporated in your backup.

Reply to the file. The "Time Machine" can be to used to restore all files at once. Tap the "Time Machine" symbol in the menu bar, and then click "Enter Time Machine". (If the "Time Machine" image is not displayed in the menu bar, please choose "Apple" menu> "System Preferences...", click "Time Machine", and then check "Show Time Machine in Menu Bar".) Hand pick One or more items that you wish to restore, then touch "Restore".

If your Macis backed up with Time Machine, you can regain your files when the operating system or startup disk is marred. To do this, you must reinstall macOS on your Mac before using Time Machine to back up and restore files.

Reinstall macOS. Your operating system files are different from personal files and will be kept on the archived system disk. However, some actions such as erasing or accidentally damaging the disk require you to restore your MacBook Pro. You can reinstall macOS and use Time Machine to restore personal files from your backup. Using macOS Big Sur, there are several ways to recover Mac. You may need to install a version of macOS that is newer than the version that came with your computer, or a version that was used before your disk was damaged.

ATTENTION: Advanced users may want to create a bootable installer to reinstall macOS in the future. If you want to use a specific version of macOS, this can be quite useful.

CONNECT YOUR MAC TO THE INTERNET

In recent years, connecting to the Internet from a Mac is quite easy, whether at home, at work, or on the road. There are two common ways to connect to the network: Wi-Fi (wireless) or Ethernet (wired) connection. If neither, you may be able to use "Instant Hotspot".

Use Wi-Fi

When a Wi-Fi network is available on the Mac, Wi-Fi image 📶 will be displayed in the menu bar at the top of the screen. Click on the image and select a network to join. If you see a lock image 🔒 next to the network name, it means that the network is protected by a password and you need to enter the password to use the Wi-Fi network.

Use Ethernet

You can use Ethernet, through Ethernet or DSL or cable modem. If an Ethernet network is available, please connect the Ethernet cable to the Ethernet port on the Mac, look for this symbol ⟨•••⟩ . If your Mac does not include a built-in Ethernet port, you can use a converter to connect the Ethernet cable to the USB or Thunderbolt port on your computer.

Use "Instant Hotspot"

If you are unable to connect to Wi-Fi or Ethernet, you may be able to use your Mac and "Instant Hotspot" to connect to the Internet through the personal hotspot on your iPhone or iPad.

When at work, while on the road or at work.

At home: Your ISP may provide Wi-Fi or Ethernet Internet connection. If you are not sure what type of connection permission you have, please ask your ISP.

At work: You may have Wi-Fi or Ethernet connection. Ask the company's IT department or network administrator for details on how to

14

connect to the company's network and usage rules.

While on the road: You can use Wi-Fi hotspots (a wireless network open to the public) or "Instant Hotspots" on your Mac (if your Mac and phone's network provider support this function). Please note that some Wi-Fi hotspots need to enter a password, agree to the terms of service or pay for use.

HOW TO USE TOUCH ID ON MAC

If your Mac is equipped with Touch ID , you can use it to unlock your Mac, authorize purchases from the iTunes Store, App Store or Apple Books, or use Apple Pay to shop online. Touch ID can be used to sign in to some third-party apps.

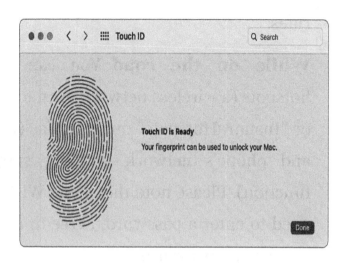

Touch ID is Ready
Your fingerprint can be used to unlock your Mac.

Set up Touch ID

- On Mac, select the "Apple" menu > "System Preferences..." and click Touch ID.
- Select "Add Fingerprint", key in your password, and follow the on-screen instructions.
  up to three fingerprints can be added to your user account (up to five fingerprints in total can be stored by your mac).

- Click the checkbox to choose how you use Touch ID:

  I. Unlock your Mac: When you wake your Mac from sleep, use Touch ID to unlock it.

  II. Apple Pay: Use Touch ID to complete purchases made with Apple Pay on this Mac.

  III. iTunes Store, App Store and Apple Books: Use Touch ID to complete your purchases from the Apple online store on this Mac.

  IV. Automatically fill in passwords: When using Safari and other apps, use Touch ID to automatically fill in user names and passwords, and automatically fill in credit card information when necessary.

Rename or delete fingerprint

On Mac, select the "Apple" menu > "System Preferences..." and click Touch ID.

Do any of the following:

- Rename the fingerprint: Click the text below the fingerprint and enter the name.
- Delete fingerprint: Click the fingerprint, enter your password, click "OK", and then click "Delete".

Use Touch ID to unlock Mac, log in or switch users

To use Touch ID for these operations, you must enter your password and be logged in to your Mac.

- Open your Mac and items protected by password: When you wake your Mac from sleep or open items protected by password, please place your finger directly on Touch ID when requested by the system.
- Sign in from the login window: touch your name in the login window, and then place your finger on Touch ID.

Only user accounts with a password can be unlocked with Touch ID. Sharing-only users and guest accounts cannot use Touch ID.

- Switch User: In the menu bar , click on the Fast User Switching menu ⊙ , select another user, then put your finger on Touch ID.

To switch to another user using Touch ID, you need to have set up fast user switching , and the user you want to switch to must have entered a password to log in to the Mac.

Use Touch ID to purchase items

- Enter the password to log in to the Mac.
- Use Apple Pay or purchase items from one of the online Apple stores.
- Place your finger on Touch ID when requested by the system.

If you encounter problems when using Touch ID

If Touch ID cannot recognize your fingerprint: Please make sure your finger is clean and dry, and then try again. Moisture, lotion, cuts or dry skin may affect fingerprint recognition.

You may still need to enter a password For security reasons, you need to enter a password when you start using your Mac. Sometimes you need to enter a password to continue using Touch ID. For instance, users must re-enter their password every 48 hours and after five wrong fingerprint identification attempts.

Note: To improve security, only the logged-in user can access their own Touch ID data, and the administrator cannot change another user's Touch ID preferences or fingerprint.

KEEP YOUR MAC UP TO DATE

Apple will regularly release macOS software updates (which may include updates of the App included with the Mac and important security updates).

If you receive a message that there is a software update, you can choose when to install the update or select to remind you the next day. You can also manually check for macOS updates in the "Software Update" system preferences.

ATTENTION: To check the update items of the software you downloaded from the App Store, please open the App Store.

Manually check Mac update items

To install update manually on your Mac, performany of the following:

- To download macOS software updates, please select the "Apple" menu > "System Preferences..." and click "Software Update".

  Tip: You can also click the Apple menu. If there are any available update items, the number will be displayed next to "System Preferences...". Select "System Preferences..." to continue.

- To update the software downloaded from the App Store, please click the "Apple" menu. If there are any available update items, the number will be displayed next to the App Store. Select App Store to continue in App Store App.

Set Mac to check for automaticsoftware updates

- On your device or Mac, click on the "Apple" menu > "System Preferences..." and touch "Software Update".

- If you want to automatically install macOS updates, please select "Keep my Mac up to date automatically".

- To set advanced update options, click "Advanced" and do any of the following:

  I. If you want your Mac to automatically check for updates, select "Check for updates".

  II. If you want Mac to download updates automatically without asking, please select "Download new updates when available".

  III. If you want your Mac to automatically install macOS

updates, select "Install macOS updates".

IV. If you want your Mac to automatically install App Updates from the App Store, select "Install App Updates from the App Store".

V. If you want your Mac to automatically install system files and security updates, please select "Install system data files and security updates".

- Click "OK".

If you want to receive the latest updates automatically, it is recommended that you select "Check for updates", "Download new updates when available" and "Install system data files and security updates".

ATTENTION: MacBook, MacBook Pro and MacBook Air must be connected to a power adapter and plugged into a power source to automatically download updates.

HOW TO TRANSFER YOUR DATA TO YOUR NEW MAC PRO

It's easy to transfer your data and settings from another Mac or PC to your Mac Pro. It is possible to transfer data from an older computer – or possibly a Time Machine backup on a USB storage device - to your Mac Pro. The transmission can be done either wirelessly or via Ethernet cable and adapter.

On an older computer You may need to update the macOS version first before you can transfer information to it. The migration assistant requires macOS 10.7 or newer. However, it is recommended that you always update an older computer to the latest version that is compatible with it.

Tip: Make sure your Mac Pro has the latest version of macOS for best results. Open the system settings and click on "Software update" to check for updates.

Wireless transmission. Use Setup Assistant to transfer the data the first time you set up your Mac Pro. If you want to transfer the data later, you can use the migration assistant. Unlock a Finder window and select Applications> Utilities. Then double click on "Migration Assistant" to start a wireless migration. Follow the instructions that appear. Make sure both computers are connected to the same network and will be next to each other throughout the migration.

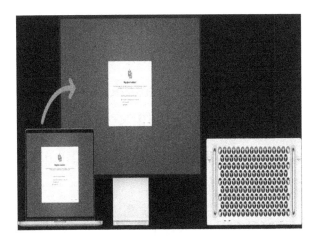

ATTENTION: The timeliest migration is when you connect your old computer to the Mac Pro by means of a cable, like a Thunderbolt 3 (USB-C).

If you used Time Machine to back up files from another Mac to a storage device (such as an external hard drive), you can copy the files from the device to your Mac Pro.

Copy files from a storage device. Connect the device to the USB 3 ⚡ or Thunderbolt 3 (USB-C) port ⚡ on the Mac Pro, then move the files from your storage device to the Mac Pro.

MANAGE FILES IN BATCHES ON MAC

You can use stacks on your desk to group files and organize them. Whenever you save a file on the desktop, it is automatically added to the appropriate batch. This way, your desk will stay clear and tidy. In the dock, a "Downloads" stacks is to group files that you upload from the Internet.

USING STACKS ON THE DESK

You can group stacks by type (such as images or PDFs), by date (such as "Creation Date" or "Last Opened"), or by Finder Tags. For example, all documents on your desk can be grouped in one pile and screenshots in a different pile.

On Mac, perform any of the following:

- Activate Batch : Click on the desktop and choose View> Use Batch or press Control-

Command-o. You can also Control-click the desktop and select Use Batch.

- Browse files in a stack: scroll left or right across the stack with two fingers on the trackpad or one finger on the Magic Mouse. It is also possible to double-click the top file in a batch to open it.

- Unlock or close a stack: tap the stack. double-click to open files.

- Alter the grouping of stacks: tap the desktop, select View> Group Stacks By, then choose one of the available options, such as Added On. You can also Control-click the desktop, "Group Batches By," then select the option you want.

- Change the appearance of stacks: Click the desktop, choose View> Show View Options, then choose the option you want. Or click while holding down the "ctrl" key on the desktop and select "Show display options". You can change the icon size or the spacing between the icons, move the icon name to a different location, or display additional information (such as the number of files in a stack).

Using stacks in the dock

The "Downloads" stack is already located in the dock by default, through which you can easily access objects that you have downloaded from the Internet, received as attachments or via AirDrop.

for quick accessYou can addfolders and files to the Dock. They can also be viewed as a stack. Your Mac will establish an alias for the file or folder.

On Mac, perform any of the following:

- Add files and folders: Drag and drop a file or folder to the right of the dividing line (after recently used apps, as shown in the illustration)

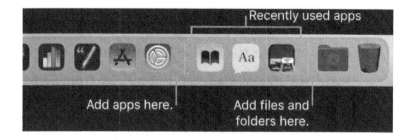

- Unlock or close a file or folder: tap it. If a folder is open, it is possible to open the objects in it by double-clicking it. Touch "Open in Finder" to indicate a folder in the Finder.

- Change the appearance of folders: Control-click the folder and choose how the items in the folder should be sorted, whether the folder should appear in the Dock as a folder or a stack, and how its contents should be displayed (for example as a grid or as a fan).

CHANGE THE LANGUAGE USED BY THE MAC

Every Mac is preconfigured to use the language of the country or region in which it is purchased. But you can always choose and use a different language. For example, if you buy your Mac in the US but prefer to use French, you can switch your Mac to French.

for individual appsYou can choose varied languages. For instance, if Simplified Chinese is your system language, but you prefer to use a particular app in English, you can do so.

Change system language

- Select "Apple" on your Mac > "System Settings" and tap "Language & Region".
- Click on "General".
- Perform one of the following:

i. Add a language: Click on "Add", select one or more languages from the list and then click on "Add".

The list is divided into two parts by a dividing line. The languages above the dividing lines are system languages that are fully supported by macOS and for menus and messages. Websites, etc. are used. The languages beneath the dividing line are not completely supported by macOS, however it may be supported by apps you work with and used for their notifications,on some websites and menus.

If you cannot use the input source selected in the input menu for input in the selected language, a list of available sources is displayed. If you don't want to add an input source immediately, you can do so later in the "Input Sources" area of the "Keyboard" system preference .

ii. Change primary language: Select a different language from the list of languages.

If macOS or an app supports the primary language, that language is used for the menus and messages. If this language is not supported, the next unselected language in the list is used, and so on. The language can also be used on websites that support the language.

The order of the languages in the list determines how text appears when you enter characters in a script that belongs to more than one language.

If you have multiple users on your Mac and you want everyone to see your chosen primary language in the login window, you can click the action menu and select "Apply to Login Window".

Select the language used for individual apps

- Select "Apple" on your Mac > "System Settings" and tap "Language & Region".

- Click on "Apps".

- Perform one of the following:

i. Select a language for an app: tap the Add button ✛ , select an app and language from the pop-up menus, and tap Add.

ii. Change the language for an app in the list: Choose an app, then choose a new language from the pop-up menu.

iii. Remove an app from the list: Select the app and click the "Remove" button ⎯ . The app uses the standard language again.

If the app is open, you may need to close and reopen it to see the change.

USE MACOS KEYBOARD SHORTCUTS

You can use key combinations (called keyboard shortcuts) to speed up operations on your Mac. Keyboard shortcuts include one or more change keys (such as Caps Lock or Control) and a last key, which you need to press at the same time. For example, you can press Command + N instead of using the pointer to move to the menu bar to select "File"> "New Window".

You can disable or change keyboard shortcuts to make them simple to use.

Explore macOS keyboard shortcuts

In macOS App, keyboard shortcuts are displayed next to menu items. Many keyboard shortcuts are standardized among different apps.

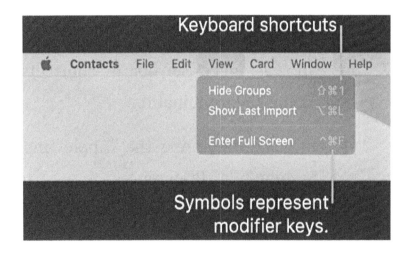

Use keyboard shortcuts to perform actions

- Hold down one or more change keys (such as Caps Lock, Command, or Control), and then press the last key of the shortcut

  For example, to use the Command + V keyboard shortcut to paste the copied text, hold down the Command key and press the V key at the same time, then release the two keys.

Customize keyboard shortcuts

You can customize keyboard shortcuts by changing the key combination.

- On your Mac, press the "Apple" menu > "System Preferences...", touch "Keyboard", and then tap "Shortcut Keys".
- Select a category in the list on the left, such as "Command Center" or Spotlight.
- In the list on the right, tick the check box next to the shortcut key you want to change.

- Double-tap the current key combination, and then touch the new key combination you prefer to use.

  In the key combination, a key (for example: letter key) can only be used once.
- Exit and reopen any apps you are using to make the new keyboard shortcuts take effect.

If you specify other commands or keyboard shortcuts that the App already has, your new shortcuts will not work. Please find the menu command that is using it, and reassign the keyboard shortcut for the item.

If you want to restore all the shortcut keys to their original key combinations, go to the "Shortcut Keys" panel of the "Keyboard" preferences and click "Restore Defaults".

Disable keyboard shortcuts

Keyboard shortcuts for apps sometimes conflict with keyboard shortcuts for macOS. If this happens, you can disable macOS keyboard shortcuts.

- On mac, touch the "Apple" menu > "System Preferences...", touch "Keyboard", and then tap "Shortcut Keys".
- Select a category in the list on the left, such as "Command Center" or Spotlight.
- In the list on the right, uncheck the check box next to the shortcut key you want to disable.

Keyboard shortcuts on Mac

You can press keyboard shortcuts to perform tasks on your Mac Pro that you would normally use a trackpad, mouse, or other device to do. the most common keyboard shortcuts are given below.

Command-X>>Cut the selected object and copy it to the clipboard.

Command-C>>Copy the selected object to the clipboard.

Command-V>>Paste the contents of the clipboard into the current document or current app.

Command-Z>>Undo previous command. Press Command-Z again to repeat.

Command-A>>Select all objects.

Command-F>>Open search window or find objects in a document.

Command-G>>Find the next occurrence of the searched object. To locate the earlier occurrence, tap Command-Shift-G.

Command-H>>Hide the app's window in the foreground. To bring the app to the foreground and hide all other apps, press Command-Option-H.

Command-M>>Place the miniature of the window in the foreground in the dock. To zoom out of all windows of the app in the foreground press "Command-Option-M".

Command-N>>Open a new document or window.

Command-O>>Open the selected object or dialog window to select a file to be opened.

Command-P>>Print the current document.

Command-S>>Save current document.

Command-W>>Close the window in the foreground. Tap "Command-Option-W" to shut down all windows of the app.

Command-Q>>Exit current app.

Command-Option-Esc>>Select the app to exit immediately.

Command tab>>Switch to the last used app under all open apps.

Command-Shift-5>>Open the "Screenshot" app. screenshots can be taken with the use of the following shortcuts:

Tap Command-Shift-3 to take a picture of the full screen.

To photograph a selected area on the screen, press Command-Shift-4.

APPLE ID ON MAC

Apple ID allows you to access iCloud, Apple Books, App Store, iTunes Store, and many other Apple services. It is composed of an email address (for example: michael_cavanna@icloud.com) and a password.

You can use an existing email address to create an Apple ID, or obtain an iCloud email address created specifically for you.

An Apple ID can be created on your iPadOS, iOS or Mac device or on the Apple ID account website.

Create an Apple ID using an existing email address or an iCloud email address generated specifically for you:

On Mac, open the "Apple" menu > "System Preferences..." and tap "Login".

Please touch "Create Apple ID" and obey instructionson the screen.

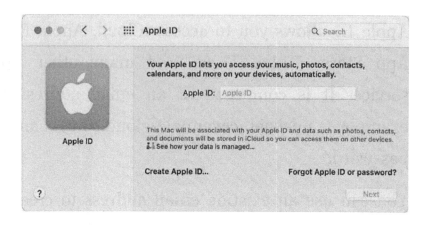

ALERT: you can use a phone number rather than an email address as your Apple ID In some countries and regions,.

To protect the security of your purchases and access to Apple services, please do not share your Apple ID and password with others. If you want to share your purchases with family members, you can set up a "family sharing" group that can join up to six family members.

SET APPLE ID PREFERENCES ON MAC

Your Apple ID allows you to access all Apple services, including iTunes Store, "Bookstore", App Store, iCloud and other Apple services.

Use the following sidebar items on the Mac to set Apple ID preferences:

- Overview: Use these options to view Apple ID and privacy policies and log out of Apple ID.

- Email, Phone and Name: you can Use these alternatives to enter your phone number, name, email information, and other contact information related to your Apple ID.

- Password and Security: these options can be used to change the password and security settings related to the Apple ID.

- Payment and mailing: Use these options to set the password and security settings connected to the Apple ID.

- iCloud: Use these options to select the iCloud features you want and manage iCloud storage space.

- Media and purchases: Use these options to change the settings of media and purchases linked to your Apple ID.
- Trusted devices: you can use this catalog to view trusted devices that employ your Apple ID, and choose and alter options for trusted devices.

If you need to use iOS or iPadOS devices to change Apple ID account settings, please refer to the "Manage Apple ID and iCloud Settings" in the iPhone , iPad or iPod touch user manual.

SET UP ICLOUD FUNCTION ON MAC

After logging in to your Apple ID , you can choose the iCloud function you want to use at any time.

Important: To set up iCloud "Messages" to share all your messages on different devices, please open "Messages" on your Mac, select "Messages"> "Preferences...", click iMessage, and then tick " Enable iCloud cloud messaging" check box.

Turn iCloud function on or off

On Mac, select the "Apple" menu > "System Preferences...", click Apple ID, and select iCloud in the sidebar.

Choose the App that has the iCloud function you want to use. Deselect any apps that you do not want to use iCloud features.

Some functions have additional settings that you can change. When the function is activated, click "Options" or "Details" near the function name.

If your "Contacts" App is synchronized with "Google Contacts", after selecting the "Contacts" function, the synchronization with Google will be turned off. If you use iCloud to sync your contacts, you should keep Google sync off.

Turn on "iCloud Photos"

On Mac, select the "Apple" menu > "System Preferences...", click Apple ID, and select iCloud in the sidebar.

Select "Photo".

Change "iCloud Keyring" option

If your Apple ID is equipped with two-factor authentication , its setting has been completed when you select "iCloud Keyring" in the iCloud App list. When you set up iCloud on a new device, you can allow the device to use iCloud data by entering the login password of the device that has been configured with iCloud.

If the "Options" button appears next to the "iCloud Keyring" option, please follow the instructions below.

- On your device, click on the "Apple" menu > "System Preferences...", touch Apple ID, and choose iCloud in the sidebar.
- Click the "Options" button next to the "Keyring" and select any of the following options:
  - I. Can your iCloud security code be used to recognize the "iCloud Keyring" on the new device.
  - II. After using the iCloud security code, the iCloud security code or phone number used to verify identity.
- If "Waiting for permission" is displayed under "Keyring", click "Options" to enter the "iCloud

Security Code" instead of approving the Mac from another device.

Change the details of "Find My Mac"

On Mac, select the "Apple" menu > "System Preferences...", click Apple ID, and select iCloud in the sidebar.

If "Location Services Disabled" is displayed under "Find My Mac", click "Details" and follow the on-screen instructions so that you can locate this Mac .

USE "ICLOUD DRIVE" TO STORE FILES ON MAC, IPHONE AND IPAD

With "iCloud Drive", you can safely store various files in iCloud and access them from all your computers, iOS and iPadOS devices. If you want, you can automatically save all files in the "Desktop" and "Documents" folders in "iCloud Drive". In this way, you can store the files directly in the location you would normally save, and they will be available on all your computers, iOS and iPadOS devices.

You can use it on Mac computers, iOS devices, iPadOS devices, and Windows computers with "iCloud for Windows". iCloud Drive". You must use the same Apple ID to log in on all computers and devices.

You can also use iCloud Drive on iCloud.com through a web browser on a Mac or Windows computer.

Set up iCloud Drive

If you haven't set up "iCloud Drive" on this Mac, you can immediately do it in the iCloud panel of iCloud preferences.

- On Mac, select the "Apple" menu > "System Preferences...", click Apple ID, and select iCloud in the sidebar.
- Select "iCloud Drive".

When you select the "iCloud Drive" function on any of your devices for the first time, you will be asked to upgrade. After the upgrade, the files and data currently stored in iCloud will be moved to iCloud cloud drive. If the system does not ask if you want to upgrade, it means that your account has been upgraded.

Important: After upgrading to "iCloud Drive ",the files stored in "iCloud Drive " can only be accessed on computers, iOS and iPadOS devices that meet the minimum system requirements , and "iCloud Drive" must be enabled. The files you have in "iCloud Drive" are also available on iCloud.com.

If you have turned off "iCloud Drive" on your device, the files and data on these devices will not be updated with those on other devices that have "iCloud Drive" enabled.

Save the "Documents" and"Desktop" folders to iCloud Drive

- On Mac, select the "Apple" menu > "System Preferences...", click Apple ID, select iCloud in the sidebar, and click "Options" next to "iCloud Drive".
  If you don't see "Options" next to "iCloud Drive", please make sure that "iCloud Drive" is enabled.
- Select "Desktop and Document Folder".
- Click "Finish".

After you select "Desktop and Document Folders", your "Desktop" and "Documents" folders will be moved to "iCloud Drive". They will also appear in the "iCloud Drive" area of the Finder sidebar .

If you can't move or save files to iCloud Drive

If you cannot move files or save files to iCloud Cloud Drive, your iCloud storage space may be full. The file stays on the Mac and uploads to iCloud Drive when space becomes available.

"ICloud Drive" will share your iCloud storage space with items such as "iCloud Photos", iOS and iPadOS device backups, and "iCloud Mail" (your @icloud.com email) mail and attachments.

To get more space, please do the following:

- Upgrade storage space.
- Wipe out items you don't wish to store in "iCloud Drive".

MANAGE ICLOUD STORAGE SPACE ON MAC

When you log in with your Apple ID and open iCloud preferences, you will automatically get 5 GB of free storage space. Your iCloud storage space is used to store files in "iCloud Drive", "iCloud Photos", iOS and iPadOS device backups, mails and attachments in "iCloud Mail" (your @icloud.com email account), etc. project. If you run out of storage space, you can upgrade the storage space. You can also remove stored items to make more free space.

View and manage iCloud storage

- On Mac, select the "Apple" menu > "System Preferences...", click Apple ID, and select iCloud in the sidebar.
- Touch "Manage" and performany of the following:
  I. Upgrade storage space: Click "Buy more storage space" or "Change storage space plan", select the storage space you want, and then follow the instructions.

When you purchase an iCloud storage upgrade, a bill will be sent to your Apple ID account. If you are in the "Family Sharing" group and you use the same Apple ID to share family purchases, the upgraded bill will be sent to the family organizer's account.

II. Check how apps and features use storage space: select an app or feature on the left, and then read the usage data on the right.

III. Remove iOS or iPadOS device backup: Click "Backup" on the left, select the device you don't need to back up on the right, and click "Delete" (located below the backup list). If you cannot see "Backup" on the left, it means that your iOS or iPadOS device does not have an iCloud backup.

Warning: If you delete the iCloud backup of the current iOS or iPadOS device, iCloud will stop automatically backing up the device.

IV. Turn off Siri and remove Siri-related data: Select Siri on the left, and then click "Disable and delete...".

- Click "Finish".

Delete items from iCloud storage

You can permanently remove all files and data in the App, remove individual files, and restore files you have deleted from "iCloud Drive" in the past 30 days. Save a copy of the file before removing it from iCloud.

CHAPTER TWO

MAC PRO OVERVIEW

Your Mac Pro is packed with many advanced technologies.

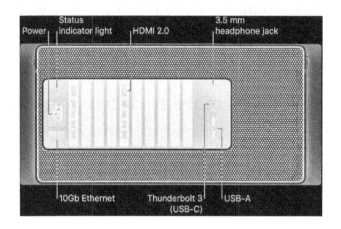

Power button : click the power button to activate your Mac Pro. (Choose the Apple menu > Shut Down to turn off the Mac Pro or the Apple menu > Hibernate to put it to sleep.)

3.5mm headphone jack: Connect stereo headphones or speakers for high quality sound while listening to music or watching movies. Or connect an analog headset with a built-in mono microphone for audio and video calls.

USB A ports (USB-3): Connect an iPad, iPhone, iPod, digital camera, external storage device, or printer. The Mac Pro's USB A ports support USB 3 and USB 2 devices up to 5 Gbps.

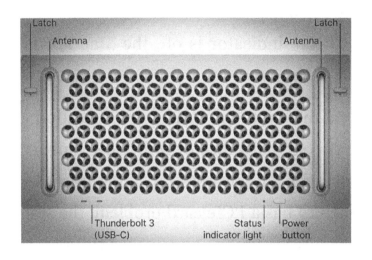

Thunderbolt 3 (USB-C) port: The Mac Pro has two Thunderbolt 3 (USB-C) ports on the front and two ports on the back. If an Apple MPX module is installed, there may be additional ports. Use these connectors to transfer data and attach docking stations and RAID arrays. The ports support screens when an Apple MPX module is installed. The ports also support USB 3 at speeds up to 10 Gbps and allow

devices such as an iPad or a rechargeable trackpad or keyboard to be charged.

Status indicators : One indicator is on the front of the Mac Pro next to the power button and another on the back of the Mac Pro next to the power connector. A solid white light indicates that the Mac Pro is on or asleep. If the indicator is off, the Mac Pro is turned off.

Note: In the event of a memory detection or data error, the status indicator will glow amber for 0.2 seconds, with this process repeating every second. If the Mac Pro has a PCIe card problem, the status light will blink twice amber and repeat the process until the computer is turned off.

HDMI 2.0 ports: The Mac Pro is capable of furnishing one or extra HDMI 2.0 ports, based on its GPU configuration. Use the ports to connect your Mac Pro to a TV or external display.

10 Gigabit Ethernet ports (RJ-45): The Mac Pro is equipped with two 10 Gb Ethernet ports that use Nbase-T Ethernet technology that provide multiple data rates for speeds of up to 10 Gbps over standard

twisted-pair copper cables with a length of up to 100 m. Depending on the devices to which the connection is to be established, the type of cable used and the technology as well as the cable length, the highest possible connection speed is negotiated automatically. For instance, if the device that are to be connected is suitable for a 10 Gbit / s and the cable favors this speed, the two devices adjust to a speed of 10 Gbit / s.

Power connector : Connect the power cord to the power connector on the back of the Mac Pro. Then connect the other end of the cable to an electrical outlet.

Power button: click on the power button to activate your Mac Pro. Select Apple menu > Shut Down to disable your Mac Pro, or press Apple menu > Sleep to put it to sleep.

KEYBOARD

The function keys on your Magic Keyboard with numeric keypad provide shortcuts for common functions such as adjusting volume and screen brightness.

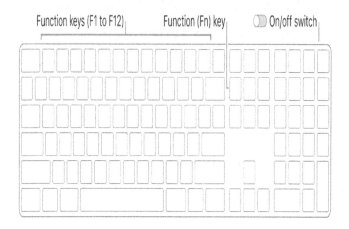

Function keys (F1 to F12)   Function (Fn) key   On/off switch

On / Off switch: Switch the keyboard on or off with the on / off switch ⬭ on the top edge of the keyboard (so that green can be seen next to the switch).

: Brightness keys (F1, F2) pressures ☼ or ☼ , to increase the brightness of the screen or decrease.

Press the "Mission Control" (F3):pressures ⊟ ,. To see what is running on your Mac Pro, including all spaces areas and open windows.

Launchpad key (F4): Press the button ⬚⬚⬚, to the launch pad to open and display all the apps on your Mac Pro immediately. Click an app to open it.

Media keys (F7, F8, F9): pressures in a song, a movie or a slide show , ◁◁ to rewind , to start or stop ▷||, or to fast forward ▷▷.

Mute button (F10): pressures ◁ , mute to the output via the built-in speakers or the 3.5mm headphone jack sound.

Volume buttons (F11, F12): Use the ◁⑴) or ◁ button to decrease or increase the volume of the sound played through the built-in speakers or the devices installed in the 3.5 mm headphone jack.

Function key (Fn): Each function key (in the top row) can also perform other functions. Hold down the Fn key while pressing a function key to perform the action assigned to that key.

TIP: Press the function key (Fn) twice to activate the dictation feature, which allows you to dictate text instead of writing it, e.g. in the apps "Messages", "Mail", "Pages" and many other apps. (Requires an external microphone)

Define keyboard settings. Click in the system settings to "keyboard" and then on top of the keys to the available options display).

Information about keyboard shortcuts. You can press keyboard shortcuts to perform tasks on your Mac Pro that you would normally use a trackpad, mouse, or other device to do.

MOUSE

Below are some common gestures you can use with your Magic Mouse 2.

Switching the mouse on and off : Switch the mouse on and off with the on / off switch on the underside of the mouse (so that green can be seen next to the switch).

Click : Press the top of the mouse surface to click or double-click.

Secondary click (i.e. right click): Press the left or right side of the mouse to make a secondary click . (In the system settings, click on "Mouse" and then on "Secondary click" to activate the right and left click.) Press the "ctrl" key on the keyboard and click.

360° scrolling : Slide your finger across the surface to scroll or pan in any direction.

Screen zoom : Hold down the Control key and scroll with one finger to zoom in on items on the screen. (Click in the system settings to "Accessibility"> "Zoom"> "zoom: scroll gesture with these special keys.")

Two-finger swipe : Swipe left or right to flip through pages, photos, and more.

Customize gestures. To lay preferences and turn on gestures, tap Mouse in System Preferences, then touch the buttons at the top to view the availableoptions.

TRACKPAD

On your Mac Pro, you can use simple trackpad gestures to perform many tasks, such as scrolling web pages, zooming in or out on documents, rotating photos, and more. The Force Touch trackpad opens up completely new ways for interactivity with its pressure-sensitive surface. You also get feedback - when moving and rotating objects with the trackpad, you feel a slight vibration when they are aligned. This enables you to work more specifically.

some of the most common gestures are outlined below:

Click: Press anywhere on the trackpad. Or activate the option "Click by tapping" in the "Trackpad" preferences and just type.

Strong click: click and then press firmly. For example, you can forcefully click a word to reveal its definition. Force-clicking on an address displays a preview that you can open in the Maps app.

Secondary click (i.e. right click): Click with two fingers to open a context menu. If the option "Click by tapping" is activated, tap with two fingers. Press the Control key on your keyboard and click the trackpad.

Scroll with two fingers :Swipe up or down with two fingers to scroll .

Pinch to zoom: Drag your thumbs and fingers in and out of photos or web pages to zoom in or out.

Swipe to navigate: Swipe left and right with two fingers to flip through web pages, documents, and more - just like turning the page of a book.

Open the Launchpad: Quickly open apps in the Launchpad. Do the pinch gesture with four or five fingers, then click an app to open it.

Swipe between apps:Swiping left or right with three or four fingers jumps from one app to the next in full screen mode.

Customize gestures. In the system settings click on "Trackpad".In "Trackpad" you can:

- Learn more about the individual gestures
- Set the preferred pressure level
- Decide whether to use pressure-sensitive features
- Customize other trackpad functions

ATTENTION: If you click hard without wanting to, you can adjust the pressure in the "Trackpad" preferences. Or, change the setting of the Look Up & Recognize option from "Force click with one finger" to "Tap with three fingers".

CHARGING THE BATTERY

Magic Trackpad 2, Magic Mouse 2 and The Magic Keyboard with numeric keypad, individuallypossess an integrated rechargeable battery.

To charge the battery. Join Magic Keyboard with the Numeric Keypad or the Magic Mouse 2 (or possibly the alternative Magic Trackpad 2) to your Mac Pro utilizing the enclosed Lightning to USB-C cable. To access the charge level, select the menu bar at the top of the screen, then choose your device. If the Bluetooth symbol ⌁ is not displayed in the menu bar, click on "Bluetooth" in the system settings and then select " Show Bluetooth in the menu bar".

USE ADAPTERS WITH YOUR MAC PRO

The adapters below can be used to connect external devices and displays to the Thunderbolt 3 (USB-C) ports that is on your Mac Pro.

Thunderbolt 3 (USB-C) to Thunderbolt 2 adapter:attach the Mac Pro to Thunderbolt display or Thunderbolt 2 devices.

USB-C Digital AV Multiport Adapter: Connect your Mac Pro to an HDMI device and a standard USB device at the same time.

USB-C to VGA Multiport Adapter: Connect your Mac Pro to a VGA projector and attach to a USB device simultaneously.

USB-C to USB-A adapter: employ a USB-C port to attach your Mac Pro to a USB-A device.

USB-C to SD card reader: Install an SD card to move high-definitionvideos and photos to your Mac Pro.

ITEMS IN THE MENU BAR ON MAC

The menu bar is located at the top of the Mac screen. Use the menus and images in the menu bar to select commands, perform tasks, and view status.

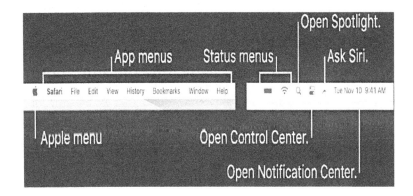

You can set the option to automatically hide the menu bar so that it will only appear when you move the pointer to the top of the screen.

"Apple" menu

"Apple" menu , Will be displayed in the upper left corner of the screen and include commands you frequently perform, such as updating the app, opening "System Preferences", locking the screen, or shutting down your Mac.

App menu

App selection unit is next to the "Apple" menu. The name of the App you are using will be shown in bold, followed by other menus, usually containing standard names such as "File", "Edit", "Format" or "Window". Each App has a "Help" menu, allowing you to easily obtain relevant information about using the App.

Each menu contains commands, many of which can be used in most apps. For example, the "Open" command is usually located in the "File" menu.

Status menu

Near the far right of the menu bar is the status menu , usually represented by an image, which allows you to check the status of your Mac (such as battery) or custom functions (such as keyboard brightness).

To view more details or options, click the status menu image. For example, click Wi-Fi 🛜 to view the list of available networks, or click "Display" 🖥 to turn on or off "Dark Mode" or "Night View". You can select the status menu to be displayed in the menu bar.

To rearrange the status menu, hold down the Command key while dragging the image.

Topromptlyomit the status menu, hold down the Command key while youdrag the image out of the menu bar.

Spotlight

If a Spotlight image $\mathbb{Q}$ is displayed in the menu bar, click the image to search for items on Mac and the web.

control center

Click "Control Center" image to open the "Control Center", you can access commonly used functions in them, such as AirDrop, AirPlay, "do not disturb" and so on.

Siri

When Siri image is displayed in the menu bar, click the image, ask Siri to perform some operations, such as opening a file or App, or to find items on the Mac or the Internet.

Notification Center

On the far right of the menu bar, click the date and time to open the "Notification Center", where you can view appointments, memos, weather, and other items, and review missed notifications.

THE MAC DESKTOP UNDERSTOOD

The menu bar is at the top of the screen, and the dock is at the bottom of the screen. The one lying in between is called the desktop. You can perform various operations on the desktop.

Change desktop picture

You can choose a different macOS desktop picture (the dynamic picture will automatically change continuously) or use a photo of yourself.

Change desktop appearance

A light or dark appearance can be chosen for built-in apps,the menu bar, dock anddesktop picture.

Organize files on the desktop

If you want to keep files on the desktop for easy use, you can use Stack to neatly group files on one side of the desktop by type or other criteria. Whenever you add files to the desktop, they will be automatically classified into Stacks in.

Find window on desktop

If the desktop is full of open windows, you can use the dispatch center to quickly access the desktop or view all the open items on the desktop in a simple view, so that you can easily find the window you want.

Use multiple desktops

You can create more desktop space to organize tasks on a specific desktop. For example, you can manage emails on one desktop, while using another desktop to focus on projects, and you can easily switch between the two desktops. You can even customize each desktop according to the tasks you are dealing with.

USE DOCK ON MAC

The Dock on the Mac desktop is a convenient place to access the apps and functions you use every day, such as the launch pad and the trash.

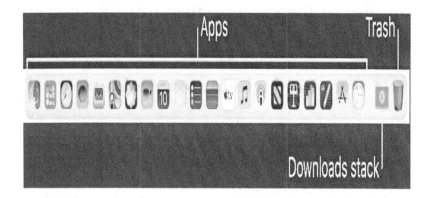

The Dock can display up to three recently used apps that have not been added to it, and one project folder downloaded from the Internet. The Dock is located at the bottom edge of the screen by default, but you can also set options to display it on the left or right edge.

Open items in the Dock

In the Dock on your Mac, perform any of the following:

- Open the App: Tap the App icon. For instance, to open the "Finder", tap the "Finder" symbol in the Dock .

- Open the file in the App: Drag the file to the App icon. For example, to access a document

70

created in Pages, move it to the Pages icon in the Dock.

- Show items in the Finder : Hold down the Command key and click the icon of the item.

- Switch to the previous App and hide the current App: Hold down Option and click the current App icon.

- Switch to another app and hide all other apps: Hold down the Option-Command key and click the app icon you want to switch to.

Perform other operations on items in the Dock

In the Dock on Mac, perform any of the following below:

- Display the shortcut menu for operations: Control-click an item to display its shortcut menu, then choose an operation (such as "Show Recent"), or click the file name to open the file.

- Force an app to quit: If the app stops responding, hold down the Control key and click the app icon, then choose "Force Quit" (unsaved changes may be lost).

remove,Add or rearrange items in the Dock

On Mac, perform any of the following:

- Add items to the Dock: move the app to the left (or above) the dividing line segregating the most newly used apps. Move the files and folders to the right (or below) the other divider that separates the most newly used apps. The avatar of the project will be placed in the dock.

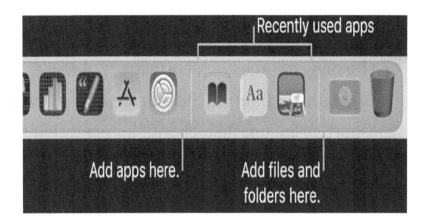

After dragging the folder to the Dock, you can view the folder by stacking the folders. The Dock usually comes with a "download" stackBy default.

- Take off an item from the Dock: move the item out of the Dock until "Remove" Is displayed. Only the alias will be removed; the real project will remain on the Mac.

  If you accidentally remove the App icon from the Dock, you can easily put it back again (the App remains on the Mac). Open the App so that its icon is displayed on the dock again. Double-click the app icon, then select "Options"> "Keep in Dock."

- Rearrange items in the Dock: Drag the item to a new location.

TIP: If you use "Relay", the "Relay" icon of the App used on iPhone, iPad, iPod touch or Apple Watch will appear near the right end of the dock.

Custom Dock

- On Mac, select   Apple menu > "System Preferences" and then tap "Dock and Menu Bar" preferences.
- In the "Dock and Menu Bar" section of the sidebar, change the options you want.
  For example, you can change the way items are displayed in the Dock, adjust the size of the Dock, place it on the left or right edge of the screen, or even hide the Dock.

To learn about the options, click the "Help" button in the panel ⊙ .

ATTENTION: To quickly adjust the size of the Dock, move the pointer to the dividing line of the Dock until the double arrow appears, then click and drag the pointer up and down. You can control-click the divider to access other actions from the shortcut menu.

keyboard shortcuts can be used to navigate to the Dock. Press Control-F3 (Control-Fn-F3 on Mac laptops) to move to the Dock. Then use the left and right arrow keys to move between the icons. Press Return to open a project.

The red mark on the icon in the Dock indicates that you need to perform one or more steps in the App or System Preferences. For example, the red mark on the "Mail" icon in the Dock indicates that you have a new email to read.

USE "CONTROL CENTER" ON MAC

The "Control Center" on your Mac allows you to quickly access macOS's main system settings, such as volume, brightness, Wi-Fi, or Do Not Disturb mode. You can customize the "Control Center" to add other items, such as accessibility shortcut keys or fast user switching.

Use "Control Center"

- On Mac, touch the "Control Center" ⊜ in menu bar
- Drag the slider (such as the "Volume" slider) or tap the icon (such as the "Airdrop" icon). To see

more options, tap anywhere in the item or tap

the arrow on the right $>$.

For example, in "Display", drag the slider to adjust the brightness of the display, or tap anywhere in "Display" to display the controls for turning "Do Not Disturb" and "Night View" on or off.

Attention: If you use an item frequently, you can drag it from the "Control Center" to the menu bar for convenient use. To omit the item from the menu bar, hold down the Command key and move it out of the menu bar.

Customize "Control Center"

- On Mac, select Apple menu > "System Preferences", and then touch "Dock and Menu Bar".

- Click a section in the sidebar to see items that are always displayed in the Control Center or items that can be added.

  I. Control Center: Items in this section will always be displayed in the Control Center and cannot be removed. Select an item in the sidebar to preview it in the "Control Center" on the right.

II.   Other modules: You can add the items in this section to the "Control Center". Select the item in the sidebar, and then select the "Show in Control Center" checkbox for that item.

To include an item in the menu bar for faster access, select the "Show in menu bar" check box for that item.You cannot add items in the "Menu bar only" section to the "Control Center".

ORGANIZING FILES IN THE FINDER ON MAC

The Finder is the foundation of your Mac. The Finder's symbol is a blue, smiling face. Tap the icon in the Dock to open a Finder window.

Finder windows let you organize and access just about anything on your Mac.

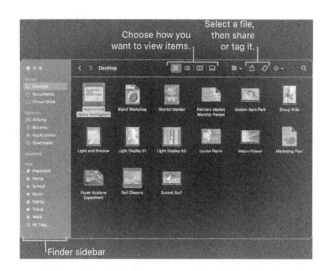

Finder sidebar

View your material

Click items in the Finder sidebar to view your files, apps, and downloads, among other things. You can customize the sidebar to make it easier for you to work with. To make the Finder window even more useful, show the preview panel.

You can also ask Siri to help you find what you're looking for.

Ask Siri. For instance say:

- "Show me all files called Expenses"
- "Show me all PDFs"

Anywhere access to everything

With iCloud Drive you can keep your iCloud files and folders. You can access these files and folders on any device where you are signed in with the same Apple ID.

Organize with folders or tags

If you want, you can organize files in folders. You can easily create new folders in your Documents folder, on the desktop or on iCloud Drive.

You can add tags with useful keywords to files and folders to make them easier to find.

Clean up a cluttered desktop

Stacks keep files neatly organized in groups on the desktop. You can group stacks by type, date or tags. When you group by type, all your images go into one stack, presentations go into another stack, and so on. All new files immediately go to the correct stack, so that everything is automatically organized.

Choose your view

You can specify how you want items to be displayed in Finder windows . This way, you don't necessarily have to list items, because the gallery view lets you visually browse your files and folders.

Send files or folders

A copy of a file or folder can be sent to a nearby iPad,iPhone or Mac or right from the Finder. Tap AirDrop in the sidebar to get started.

You can as well select a folder or file in the Finder and then touch the share ⬆️button (or use the Touch Bar) to send the file or folder via Mail, AirDrop, Messages, or another app. If the share button is not displayed, touch   the "More toolbar items" ≫button at the end of the toolbar.

Share files or folders

You can work on a file or folder on iCloud Drive with other people who use iCloud. To do this, select a file or folder in the Finder, click the share button (or use the Touch Bar), then choose Share File or Share Folder. If the share button is not displayed, tap the "More toolbar items" button at the end of the toolbar.

How to Sync data between your Mac and other compatible devices

You can connect your iPhone, iPad, or iPod touch to your Mac to transfer and update items from one device to another.

For example, if you add a movie to your Mac, you can sync the Mac with your iPhone and watch the movie on both devices. You can sync all kinds of items, such as music, movies, TV shows, podcasts and books.

Work faster with the help of key combinations

You can also use keyboard shortcuts for common actions.

USING THE MESSAGE CENTER ON THE MAC

In the message center on your Mac you can access details about your day, such as your, the weather forecast,appointments and even an outline of what's scheduled for the next day. In addition, you can read notifications you have missed.

Open or close the message center on the Mac

On your Mac, do one or more of the following:

- Open the notification center: Click the date and time in the menu bar or swipe left with two fingers from the right edge of the trackpad.
- Close the notification center: Click the desktop, click the date and time in the menu bar, or swipe right with two fingers toward the right edge of the trackpad.

Work with notifications in the message center on Mac

In the message center, hold the pointer over a notification and do one or more of the following:

- Expand or collapse a stack of notifications: If an app's notifications are grouped, the notifications are stacked. To expand the stack and see all notifications, click anywhere in the top notification. To collapse the stack again, click Show Less.

- Take immediate action: Click on the task. For instance, tap 'Snooze' in a notification from the Calendar app or touch 'Reply' in a message from the Mail app.

If there is an arrow ⌄ next to a task, click the arrow for more options. For example, to respond to a call through the Messages app, click the arrow next to "Decline" and choose "Reply with message."

- See more: Click the notification to open the item in the app. If an arrow › appears to the right of the app name , click the arrow to view details in the notification.

- Change an app's notification settings: If an arrow ⟩ appears to the right of the app name , click the arrow. Then click the More button ••• and choose an option:

  I. Deliver silently: No notifications are shown in the top right corner of the screen or the lock screen (they will appear in the message center), and there is no sound when you receive notifications.

  II. Deliver clearly: Notifications are shown at the top right of the screen and in the lock screen (and in the message center), and a beep sounds when you receive notifications.

  III. Disable: You will not receive notifications. To turn notifications back on for the app, choose Apple menu > 'System Preferences' and click 'Notifications'. Select the app on the left, then click Allow Notifications on the right (blue indicates notifications are enabled).

IV. Notifications preference pane: Displays the app's notification settings in Notifications preference pane.

- Delete a notification or all notifications in a stack: Click the 'Delete' or 'Delete all' button ⊗.

Work with widgets in the message center on Mac

In the message center, do one or more of the following:

- See more: Click anywhere in a widget to open its preferences, app or web page. For example, click anywhere in the Clock widget to open the Date & Time pane of System Preferences, or click in the Reminders widget to open the Reminders app.

- Remove a widget: Hold down the Option key while moving the pointer over the widget and click the button ⊖ with the minus sign .

Customize the message center on the Mac

- On your Mac, open Notification Center and click Edit Widgets at the bottom.
- Perform any of the following steps:
  I. Search for a widget : Use the search field to locate a widget, or tap a category, such as Clock, to preview the accessible widgets.
  II. Add a widget: In the widget preview, click a size (if available), hover over the widget in the preview image, and click the plus sign ⊕ button. The widget is then added to the active widgets on the right.
  III. Reorder widgets: Drag one of the active widgets to a different location.
  IV. To change a widget: In the active widgets, move the pointer over the widget ("Edit widget" appears below its name) and click anywhere in the widget. The widget is then flipped to show settings that you can adjust. For example, you can change the list that is displayed in the Reminders widget. Click 'Done' when you're done.

V.   Resize a widget : In the active widgets, Control-click a widget and choose a different size.

VI.   Delete an active widget: Move the pointer over an active widget and click the minus ⊖ button.

- When you're done, click Done at the bottom of the active widgets.

HOW THE IPAD CAN BE USED AS A SECOND SCREEN FOR MAC

With Sidecar, you can use your iPad in landscape mode as a second screen for your Mac. As with any other secondary screen, you can expand your desk and display other apps or windows on your iPad, or you can display the same apps and windows on your iPad as you would on your Mac.

Note: Sidecar is an integration function. To use the integration functions, WiFi and Bluetooth must be activated on your devices and your devices must meet certain system requirements.

Set sidecar options

Ensure you're logged in with the matching Apple ID on your Mac and iPad .

- Open "Apple" on your Mac > "System settings" and touch "Sidecar".
- Set options so that the sidebar and touch bar are visible on the iPad and so that the Apple Pencil can be used.

- Click on "Connect to" and select your iPad if you are not already connected to the iPad.

You can also use the Monitor option in Control Center ⊙, the Monitor menu 🖳 in the menu bar (if the menu is displayed), or the AirPlay Monitor pop-up menu in Monitors preferences.

To use Sidecaryou are not required to connect your iPad to your Mac with a cable.

Use sidecar

- If there is still no connection to your iPad, click on "Monitor" in the control center ⊙ or on the "Monitor" 🖳 menu in the menu bar (if the menu is displayed).
The "Sidecar" menu is displayed in the menu bar 🖳 faded in. In the "Sidecar" menu, you can easily change how you want to use the iPad. For example, you can choose to use iPad as a synced screen or a separate screen, and

have the sidebar or Touch Bar on the iPad show or hide.

- Do any of the following:

i. Move windows from Mac to iPad: move a window to the edge of the screen until the pointer comes up on the iPad. Alternatively, if you're using an app, select Window> Move Window To iPad.

ii. Move windows from iPad to Mac:Drag a window to the edge of the screen until the pointer appears on the Mac. Alternatively, if you're using an app, choose Window> Move Window On Mac.

iii. Sidebar on the iPad use: Tap with your finger or the Apple Edit the icons in the sidebar display to the menu bar ⎚ or hide ⎚ , display around the dock ⎚ or hide ⎚ or display the on-screen keyboard ⌨ . Alternatively, tap one or more special keys (such as the "ctrl" key ^) if you want to use keyboard shortcuts.

iv. Use the Touch Bar on the iPad: Tap any button on the Touch Bar with your finger or Apple Pencil. The buttons available depend on the app or task.

v. Use Apple Pencil on iPad: Use Apple Pencil to tap to select items such as menu commands, checkboxes, and files. In some apps, you can switch between drawing tools by double-tapping the bottom of the Apple Pencil. The prerequisite for this is that your Apple Pencil supports this function (and that you set the corresponding option in the sidecar settings).

vi. Use gestures on iPad: You can use basic gestures like tap, swipe, scroll, and zoom, as well as gestures to enter and edit text.

vii. Change between the Mac desktop and iPad on iPad: scroll up from the bottom of the iPad with one finger to display the Home screen. Swipe up and pause to see the iPad dock. Scroll up and pause in the center of the screen to reveal the app switcher. Pranks upwards and tap the sidecar symbol , if you want to return to the Mac desktop.

- When you no longer want to use your iPad, tap the Disconnect icon at the bottom of the iPad sidebar .

  You can also disconnect on your Mac by tapping the active iPad in the sidecar menu is listed in the menu bar.

CHAPTER THREE

FAMILY SHARING ON MAC

"Family Sharing" permit family members up to six to share App Store and iTunes Store without the need to share accounts. Your family can share subscription items for Apple Music, Apple TV, Apple News+ and Apple Arcade. Your family can also use the "Find" app on Mac, iCloud.com, iOS and iPadOS devices to help each other find their devices.

An adult (family organizer) can set up "Family Sharing" and invite up to five people to join the "Family Sharing" group.

- On Mac, select the "Apple" menu > "System Preferences..." and do one of the following:

    I.   If you have logged in to your Apple ID: Click "Family Sharing" .

    II. If you have not logged in to your Apple ID or do not have an Apple ID: Click "Login" and follow the instructions on the screen (enter your Apple ID, In the event that

you lack   an Apple ID, please touch
"Create Apple ID"). After logging in, click
at the top of the "System Preferences"
window ▪▪▪▪ , and then click "Family
Sharing" that appears next to Apple ID
preferences   .

- Touch "Get Started" and then implore people to
  join your "Family Sharing" group:

I.   Invite family members: Click "Invite Others"
     and follow the onscreen instructions.
     If the person you want to invite is nearby,
     you can select "Invite in person" and ask the
     person to enter their Apple ID and password
     on your Mac. Otherwise, you can use "Mail",
     "Message" or AirDrop to send the invitation.
     If the person you invite does not have an
     Apple ID, they must create an Apple ID to
     accept your invitation.

II. Create Apple ID for young children: Click
     "Create Child Account" and follow the on-
     screen instructions.

- To add more family members to the Family Sharing group, click the "Join" button $+$ and follow the instructions on the screen.
- Choose the apps and services you want to share with your family.

I. Apple Music: Select Apple Music in the sidebar. If you do not have an Apple Music subscription, please click "Learn More" to learn about Apple Music subscription items. When you subscribe to the Apple Music family membership, all family members can automatically and unlimited access to Apple Music.

II. Apple TV+: Select Apple TV+ in the sidebar. If you do not have an Apple TV+ subscription, please click "Learn More" to learn about Apple TV+ subscription items.

III. Apple Arcade (not available in some countries or regions): Select Apple Arcade in the sidebar. If you do not have an Apple Arcade subscription, please click "Learn More" to learn more about Apple Arcade subscriptions.

IV. Apple News+: Select Apple News+ in the sidebar. If you do not have an Apple News+ subscription, please click "Learn More" to learn about Apple News+ subscriptions.

V. Location Sharing: Select "Location Sharing" in the sidebar, then click "Learn More" to learn how to set up location sharing on all devices. You can set location sharing so that all family members can view each other's location in the "Find" app and "Messages". You can use the "Find" app on Mac, iCloud.com, iOS and iPadOS devices.

VI. Purchase Sharing: Select "Purchase Sharing" in the sidebar. If you have set the payment method, please click "Set up purchase sharing"; otherwise, please click "Add Payment Method" and follow the instructions on the screen. Your family can share items purchased from the iTunes Store, Apple Books, and App Store, so everyone can access them. So purchase items are all done through the shared payment method you set. You can change the account used to purchase items and refuse to share your purchases with family members.

VII.   iCloud Storage: Select "iCloud Storage" in the sidebar, and then share your existing 200GB or 2TB "iCloud Storage" plan, or upgrade to a plan you can share with "Family". Family members can share plans with you or keep their personal storage plans.

VIII.   Ask before buying: Click "Ask before buying" in the sidebar, and then click "Open inquiry before buying". The beauty of this setting is that children in the family sharing group will have to obtain your permission before they can actually purchase items from theiTunes Store, Apple Books or

App Store,

IX.   Screen usage time: Select "Screen usage time" in the sidebar, click "Open screen usage time settings", and then select the option you want.

Each family member must confirm the Apple ID used to share the iTunes Store, App Store, and Apple Books purchases before all family members can use the purchases.

LOG IN OR LOG OUT OF FACETIME ON A MAC

you need to log on to FaceTime with your Apple ID andensure that FaceTime is enabledenable you can make or receive FaceTime calls or calls on your Mac,.

Sign in to FaceTime

When you open the app for the first time or if you are logged out, you need to log in to FaceTime.

- In the FaceTime App write down your passwordand Apple ID.
- Click "Next". FaceTime will automatically turn on.

If you forget your Apple ID or password, or if you need to create an Apple ID, please go to the Apple ID account website .

Please make sure that the same Apple ID is logged on each device.

Sign out of FaceTime

After logging out of FaceTime, you have to log in again to receive FaceTime calls or phone calls.

- In the FaceTime App on your Mac, select FaceTime> "Preferences..." and click "Settings".
- Click "Sign Out".

Turn FaceTime on or off

If you want to keep FaceTime logged in but don't want to answer incoming calls, you can turn FaceTime off. If someone makes a call to you, you will not receive an incoming call notification; to the caller, it looks like you failed to answer.

Perform any of the following in the FaceTime App:

- Close FaceTime: Choose FaceTime> "Close FaceTime".
  TIP: In addition to turning off FaceTime, you can also turn on "Do Not Disturb Mode" in the

"Control Center" so that you will not be disturbed by notifications.

- Open FaceTime: Choose FaceTime> "Open FaceTime".

ATTENTION: To block all phone calls or FaceTime, please disable or log out of FaceTime on individual device. (You can also block individual callers . People in your blocked list will remain blocked on all devices that you log in to FaceTime and iCloud with the same Apple ID.)

MAKE A CALL IN FACETIME ON MAC

You can make FaceTime calls with one or more users who have a Mac, iOS device, or iPadOS device. You can only make a FaceTime call withmobile dataor Wi-Fi.

Ask Siri. You can say this:

"FaceTime Mommy"

"FaceTime Voice [Phone Number]"

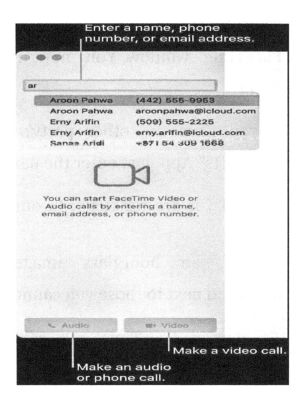

Enter a name, phone number, or email address.

Aroon Pahwa	(442) 555-9953
Aroon Pahwa	aroonpahwa@icloud.com
Erny Arifin	(509) 555-2225
Erny Arifin	erny.arifin@icloud.com
Sanaa Aridi	+871 54 309 1668

You can start FaceTime Video or Audio calls by entering a name, email address, or phone number.

Make a video call.

Make an audio or phone call.

You can also use the mobile network connection of a nearby iPhone to call anyone directly from your Mac.

Make a FaceTime call

- In the FaceTime App on the Mac , log in and make sure FaceTime is turned on .

101

- Enter the email address or phone number you want to call in the field at the top of the FaceTime window. You may need to press Return.

  If you have the other party's card in your "Contacts" App, just enter the name.

  Note: If you are restricted to only talk to some people, an hourglass image will be displayed next to those you cannot talk to.

- To start a FaceTime call, click the "video" button or the "Voice" button (or use the "touch bar").

  If you click the "Voice" button and you have set the phone can be played on a Mac , you can choose to play a voice call or FaceTime calls. The camera will automatically turn off during voice or mobile phone calls.

- After the call is connected, you can change the way the call is displayed , pause the call , mute the call or change the volume , or add more users to the FaceTime call .

If your video call rejected or turned on, you can click the "Messages" button to send iMessage to the other party (the parties are required to sign in to iMessage).

Make a "Group FaceTime" call

You can call up to 32 people at the same time during a "Group FaceTime" call.

- In the FaceTime App on the Mac , log in and make sure FaceTime is turned on .
- Enter the email address or phone number you want to call in the field at the top of the FaceTime window. You may need to press Return.

If you have the other party's card in your "Contacts" App, just enter the name.

ATTENTION: If you are restricted to only talk to some people , an hourglass image will be displayed next to those you cannot talk to.

Repeat step 2 until all members are listed.

- To start a FaceTime call, click the "video" button or the "Voice" button (or use the "touch bar").

If you click the "Voice" button and you have set the phone can be played on a Mac , you can choose to play a voice call or FaceTime calls. The camera will automatically turn off during FaceTime voice or phone calls.

Each member will be displayed in a box on the screen. When a member speaks, or you click a box, the box will move to the front and become more obvious. Blocks that cannot be placed due to insufficient screen space are displayed in rows at the bottom of the screen. To find members you can't see, scroll the row to view them.

ATTENTION: If you don't want the speaker's square to become larger, you can deselect this option in FaceTime preferences. Choose FaceTime> "Preferences...", click "Settings", and then deselect "Speaker" under "Automatic highlighting."

To send a voice prompt to callers who have not yet joined the call, click the "Sidebar" ⊟button , and then click "Call".

After the call is connected, you can change the way the call is displayed , pause or mute the call or change the volume .

Add more users to FaceTime calls

In a FaceTime call, even if the call is not made by you, you can add more users to the call (up to 32 other users).

- In the FaceTime App on Mac , make or participate in FaceTime calls or "group FaceTime" calls .
- Click the "Sidebar" ⊟button .
- Click the "Add Contact" ⊕ button and enter the email address or phone number of the person you are calling. If you have the other party's

card in your "Contacts" App, just enter the name.

ATTENTION: If you are restricted to only talk to some people , an hourglass image⧖ will be displayed next to those you cannot talk to.

- Click "Add".

Each member will be displayed in a box on the screen. When a member speaks, or you click a box, the box will move to the front and become more obvious. Blocks that cannot be placed due to insufficient screen space are displayed in rows at the bottom of the screen. To find members you can't see, scroll the row to view them.

ATTENTION: If you don't want the speaker's square to become larger, you can deselect this option in FaceTime preferences. Choose FaceTime> "Preferences...", click "Settings", and then deselect "Speaker" under "Automatic highlighting."

To send a voice prompt to callers who have not yet joined the call, click the "Sidebar" ⊟button , and then click "Call".

After the call is connected, you can change the way the call is displayed , pause or mute the call or change the volume.

End the call

In FaceTime App on Mac , perform any of the following to end the call:

- End the voice call: Click the "End" ☎button in the notification.
- End a video call: Move the cursor to the top of the call window, and then click the "End Call" ⊗button (or use the touch bar).

After you end the "Group FaceTime" call, the call will continue until all members leave. To rejoin, please click the "Add Video" button.

ANSWER INCOMING CALLS IN FACETIME ON MAC

After you log in and turn on FaceTime, you can accept or decline calls even if FaceTime is not turned on.

Answer FaceTime calls

I. On a Mac, when a notification appears in the upper right corner of the screen, perform one of the following:

- To answer the call: Click "Accept".

- To answer a video call as a voice call: Click ∨ next to "Accept" and select "Answer by voice." The camera will automatically turn off during voice or mobile phone calls.

- Answer the video or voice call, and end the current call: Click "End and Answer".

- Answer the voice call and pause the current voice call: Click "Hold and Answer". When you end a new call, the suspended call will resume. You can pause one voice call at a time.

- To join a "Group FaceTime" call: Click "Add", and then click the "Add Video" button in the FaceTime window.
- You can as well accept "Group FaceTime" calls in "Messages". When you receive a request, touch "Join" in the FaceTime message bubble.

II. During a call, you can perform any of the following operations:

- Change how calls are displayed
- Pause call
- Silent or alter the volume of a call
- Add to address book
- Add more users to FaceTime calls

Reject FaceTime calls

On a Mac, when a notification appears in the upper right corner of the screen , do one of the following:

- Reject the call: Click "Reject".
- **ATTENTION**: If the call is from someone you don't want to answer, you can block the caller .

- Reject the call and send a message using iMessage: Click ∨ next to "Reject", select "Reply with a message" and enter the message, then click "Send". Both you and the caller must log in to iMessage.

- Decline calls and set reminders for later calls back: Click ∨ next to "Decline" and select the waiting time for you to receive reminders. When you receive a notification at the specified time, click the notification to view the reminder, and then click the link in the reminder to start the call.

If your Mac is equipped with the "Touch Bar", you can use it to answer calls, reject calls and send messages, or reject calls and set reminders.

You cannot answer calls from people who are restricted by communication restrictions in "Screen Time", but they will be displayed as missed calls in the FaceTime window or "Notification Center".

KEYBOARD SHORTCUTS IN FACETIME ON MAC

In addition to the shortcut keys displayed in the FaceTime menu, the shortcut keys you can use are listed below.

Action.   Hot key

Open FaceTime preferences>>Command + comma (,)

Hide FaceTime>>Command + H

Hide all items except FaceTime>>Option + Command + H

Turn off FaceTime>>Command + K

Quit FaceTime>>Command + Q

Close the FaceTime window>>Command + W

Shrink the window to its smallest size>>Command + M

Enter or exit the full-screen display mode during a video call>>Control + Command + F

Use landscape or portrait mode when making a video call>>Command + R

CHAPTER FOUR

SAFARI

MAKE SAFARI THE DEFAULT WEB BROWSER ON MAC: When you click on links in emails or other documents, they will open in your default browser. When you set up your Mac for the first time, Safari is the default browser, but another browser you installed may accidentally become the default browser.

On Mac, choose the "Apple" menu > "System Preferences..." and tap "General".

Hand pick the "Default Web Browser" pop-up menu and choose Safari.

Some apps use a browser other than the default browser to open web pages.

CUSTOMIZE THE SAFARI BROWSER WINDOW ON MAC

You can change the course Safari, buttons and bookmarks layout to suit your browsing habits.

Use "preference items" column

In Safari App on your Mac , select the "Display">
"display your favorite items listed."

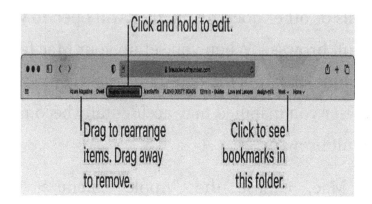

Display the status bar

In Safari App on your Mac, select the "Display">
"display the status bar." When you move the cursor to
the link on the bottom of the Safari window status
column displays the full address of the link.

Customize Toolbar

In Safari App on the Mac to perform one of the
following actions:

- Change the toolbar in the project: select "Display"> "Customize Toolbar", and then drag the toolbar item to add, remove and rearrange items. For example, you can add the "iCloud Tabs" button, it will show you the other device (enabled features in iCloud Safari preferences in) on the list of the pages have been opened.

- Quickly rearrange the toolbar buttons: Hold down the Command key and drag left and right buttons. This shortcut can not be applied to the "Previous / Next", "sidebar", "Home", "History", "downloads" button or the "Smart Search" field.

- Adjust the size of the toolbar: If you see angle brackets » in the column right tools, represents the window is too small to display all toolbar items. Please zoom window, or click in brackets, you can see the rest of the project.

- Remove toolbar items: Hold down the Command key and drag items out of the toolbar.

- Show or hide the toolbar in full-screen display mode: when full screen display, select "Display"> "is always displayed in full-screen toolbar."

To further customize Safari, select Safari> "Preferences …" and then change the options.

CHANGE PREFERENCES FOR SAFARI ON MAC

Use Safari preferences to browse the Internet in the way that suits you best.

In the Safari App on your Mac, select Safari> "Preferences..." and click on one of the preference panels:

- General : Change the content displayed when opening a new window or tab, the length of time to keep the browsing history, which bookmark to display in the favorite item display mode, and select the storage location and retention time of the downloaded item.

- Tabs : Choose when to open pages in tabs, choose to use keyboard shortcuts, and choose to display website images in tabs.

- Auto-fill : Choose to automatically fill in the previously saved contact information on the form, automatically enter the previously saved user name and password when revisiting the website, and automatically enter the previously saved credit card information on the web page.

- Password: View, add, change, remove and share your saved website username and password.

- Search: Select the search engine you want to use when searching the Internet in Safari, and choose how to use the "Smart Search" field to assist the search.

- Security: Enable warnings when you go to suspicious phishing websites, and allow websites to use JavaScript.

- Privacy: Prevent third-party content providers from tracking you across websites, block the storage of cookies on the Mac, remove some or all of the cookies stored on the Mac, allow websites to check whether you have enabled

Apple Pay, and allow Apple websites and apps Check if you have an Apple Card on your Mac.

- Website: Choose to block advertisements, prevent video playback, block pop-up items, etc. for individual websites.

- Extensions : Install Safari extensions from the Mac App Store to add custom control items, change the appearance of web content, etc.

- Advanced: show the full URL in the "Smart Search" field, establish the smallest font level for web pages, save articlesautomatically for offline reading, access tools for developing websites through the "Development" menu, etc.

To learn more about the options in the panel, click the "Help" ? button at the bottom of the panel.

BLOCK POP-UP MENUS IN SAFARI ON MAC

web pages can be prevented from showing pop-up windows.

- In the Safari App on your Mac, select Safari> "Preferences..." and click "Websites".

- Click "Pop-up Window."
- Block the following pop-up windows:
  I. Websites in the list: Select the website in the column on the right, and then choose the option you want.
  II. All websites that are not currently customized: Click the "When visiting other websites" pop-up menu in the lower right corner of the panel, and then select the options you want.
  III. You can see all the websites you have customized under "Set Sites". If you don't see the "configured website", it may be that you have not customized the website or you have cleared the list.
  IV. All websites: Make sure that there are no websites listed under "Configured websites" (to quickly clear the list, select the website and click "Remove"). Tap "When visiting other websites" pop-up menu and select the option you would prefer.

If you select "Block and notify" for the pop-up window on the website, click the image in the "Smart Search" field to display the pop-up window.

[Note] Blocking pop-up windows may also block some of the content you want to watch.

PREVENT CROSS-SITE TRACKING IN SAFARI ON MAC

Some websites use third-party content providers. You may not allow third-party content providers to track you on different websites to provide advertisements for products and services.

- In the Safari App on your Mac, select Safari> "Preferences..." and click "Privacy".
- Select "Prevent cross-site tracking".
  Unless you visit and interact with third-party content providers as a first-party website, cookies and website information will be deleted .
  Social media sites usually put "Share", "Like" or "Comment" buttons on their website. These buttons can be used to track your web browsing

activity even if you didn't click it. Safari will block such tracking. If you still want to use these buttons, you will be asked to authorize the website to view your activities on other websites.

[Note] Whenever you visit a website, the website will collect your device information, such as system settings, and use this information to display web pages applicable to your device. Some companies use this data to try to uniquely identify your device, which is called fingerprint recognition . To prevent tracking, Safari will provide a simplified version of your system settings whenever you visit a website. Your Mac will look like everyone else's Mac, which can greatly reduce the ability of the tracker to identify your device exclusively.

HOW TO MANAGE WEBSITE DATAANDCOOKIES IN SAFARI ON MAC

You can change the options in Safari preferences to allow Safari to always accept or block cookies and website data.

In the Safari App on your Mac, select Safari> "Preferences...", click "Privacy", and then do one of the following:

- Avoid trackers using cookies and website data to track you: Select "Prevent cross-site tracking".
- Cookies and website data will be deleted unless you visit and interact with the tracker's website.
- block cookiesall the time: choose "Block all cookies".
- Third parties, advertisers and Websites are unable store cookies and other data on your Mac. This may hinder some websites from working appropriately.

- allow cookies all the time: Uncheck "Block all cookies".
- third parties, advertisers and Websites, can save cookies and other information on your Mac.
- Remove stored cookies and data: Click "Manage Site Information", select one or more sites, and click "Remove" or "Remove All".
- Removing data may help to curtail tracking, but it may also log you out of the site or distort its behavior.
- Check which websites store cookies or data: Click "Manage Website Information".

[**ATTENTION**] Changing cookie preferences or removing cookies and website information in Safari may change or remove cookies in other apps.

PAYING WITH THE APPLE PAY IN SAFARI ON MAC

You can use Apple Pay to shop easily and securely in Safari on your Mac. Look for Apple Pay at checkout, and use a Mac, iPhone (iOS 10 or above) or Apple

Watch (watchOS 3 or above) with Touch ID to complete the purchase. If you use iPhone or Apple Watch to complete the purchase, you must log in with the same Apple ID as the Mac .

Before using Apple Pay, please set up a credit or debit card on the device you want to use to complete the purchase.

- In the Safari App on the Mac, during checkout, click Apple Pay.
  Before completing the purchase, you can change your credit card, shipping address, or contact information.
- Complete the purchase.
  I.   Mac with Touch ID: Place your finger on Touch ID to complete the purchase. If you haven't set up Touch ID, you can tap the "Pay" button in the touch bar and enter the password. If your Mac is not equipped with a Touch Bar or you are using a Mac equipped with an Apple chip, you can double-tap Touch ID and enter your password.

II. Only one user account on the Mac can use Touch ID to complete purchases using Apple Pay on the Mac. Other user accounts must useApple Watch or iPhone.

III. iPhone: Press the side button twice, and then use Face ID or Touch ID on the iPhone to authenticate.

IV. Apple Watch: Double-click the side button.

FILL IN CREDIT CARD INFORMATION AUTOMATICALLY IN SAFARI ON MAC

With "Auto-fill", you can fill in your formerly saved credit card information, passwords, and more. When you create a password on the website, you can also create a strong password. The fields that have been entered for you will be highlighted in yellow.

Add credit card or remove saved credit card

- In the Safari App on your Mac, select Safari> "Preferences..." and click "AutoFill".
- Choose "Credit Card", touch "Edit", and obey the instructions on the screen.

Fill in your credit card information

- In the Safari App on the Mac,click the credit card field when making a purchase.
- Select from a catalog of stored credit cards. If your Mac is equipped with Touch ID , you can use Touch ID to fill in the stored information for the selected credit card.

To ensure security, Safari does not store credit card security codes. Every time you use a credit card on a website, you must enter it manually.

If any other fields are empty or the type of datashown is untrue, touch that field, then tap the credit card image and choose the exact information (or possibly use the touch bar).

[Important] Any user who uses your Mac with your user login information, Safari will automatically fill in your information for them. If other devices and your Mac have already set up an "iCloud Keyring", it will also automatically fill in your information for anyone using your devices.

For security, please configure your Mac to display the login window when it is turned on , and ask for a password when it sleeps or when the screen saver starts . Please set your iPhone, iPad and iPod touch to require a passcode to unlock the screen.

[Reminder] If you use "iCloud Keychain" on Mac and other devices to protect the security of your information , you can use "Autofill" on all devices to enter previously stored credit card information.

Credit card information will be encrypted in your macOS keyring. If "iCloud Keyring" has been set on your Mac, it will also be encrypted in your "iCloud Keyring".

If you remove credit card information in Safari, it will be deleted from your macOS keyring. If your Mac and other devices have configured "iCloud Keychain", it will also be removed from your other devices.

CHAPTER FIVE

HOW TO CUSTOMIZE YOUR MAC

CUSTOMIZE YOUR MAC IN SYSTEM PREFERENCES: You can change system preferences to customize your Mac the way you want. For example, you can change the size and position of the dock , choose between a light and dark display mode, use a different desktop background and more.

To change the system settings of your Mac, click on the icon for the system settings in the Dock or select "Apple" > "System settings".

Explore system settings

The options for customizing your Mac are grouped together in various system settings. For example, the options you can set for Spotlight are in the Spotlight preferences.

The system settings are shown as a grid of symbols. The icons that appear depend on your Mac and the apps you have installed. Click an icon to open a system preference and view its options.

Define options in a system setting area

Each area of a system preference has options that you can choose from. Most areas have a Help button ⊘ that you can click for more information about the options.

Some areas of System Preferences are locked to protect your Mac. When the lock is closed in the lower left, click the lock to unlock System Preferences .

Find options in the system settings

Use the search box at the top of the window if you don't know where the option you want is located. Options that match your search term are listed and the System Preferences area in which they are located is highlighted.

Adjust system settings

- Hide a system setting: Choose View> Customize, deselect the System Settings box, and click Done at the top of the window.
- Show hidden system settings : Choose "View"> "Customize", activate the field for the hidden system settings and click on "Done" at the top of the window.
- Rearrange system settings: Choose "View"> "Sort by Category" or "Sort alphabetically".

If you see a red mark on the System Preferences icon in the Dock, you need to take one or more actions. For example, if you haven't fully configured iCloud, the badge will appear on the icon in the Dock. When you click the icon, System Preferences will open so you can complete the configuration.

If you want to change the options of an app such as Mail or Safari, open the app, click on the name of the app in the menu bar and select "Settings". There are no system settings for some apps.

CHANGE THE DESKTOP BACKGROUND ON YOUR MAC

You can choose the image that appears on the desk. Your Mac comes standard with several dozen desktop wallpapers that you can choose from. But it is also possible to use your own photos or monochrome background images.

ATTENTION: You can drag a picture from your desk or folder onto the thumbnail at the top of the area to use that picture as your desk picture.

- Hand pick "Apple" on Mac > "System Settings", touch "Desktop & Screensaver" and then on "Desktop".
- Select an image or color on the left:
  i. Pictures and colors that are available by default on your Mac: Click on the arrow ⟩next to "Apple" and select a folder , e.g. For example, "Desk", "Pictures" or "Colors" to see thumbnails of the available pictures or colors.

     Depending on your current location, dynamic desktop images can change automatically over the course of the day. If location services have been disabled in the Security preferences , the image will change based on the time zone you specified in the Date & Time preferences.

     Some dynamic desktop images may also offer still images so that the desktop image does not detract from the light or dark appearance of the desk. For example, if you select dark mode while configuring macOS, a dark still image is used as the desktop background. Click the pop-up menu and choose the appropriate option to use or stop using a still image, if available.

ii. Your pictures: Click the arrow next to "Photos" (or "iPhoto" if available). If your pictures are in the "Pictures" folder or another folder, click the arrow next to "Folder" and select a folder.

To add a folder, click Add ,navigate to the folder, and select the folder. Then click on "Select".

If you don't see anything after selecting the folder that contains your pictures, the pictures may not be in the correct format (JPEG, PICT, TIFF, PNG, or HEIC). To change the image format, open the image in the preview and save it in the new format. Use larger images (higher resolution such as 1024 x 768 pixels) if your images look fuzzy and blurry.

- click twice on the image you would love to use.

The desktop background changes instantly and you can see what the picture looks like. If you're using your own image, you can choose to fill the entire screen, display it in the middle, or place it elsewhere. Just click on different pictures and try out pictures and arrangements until you like the ad.

If you want to use all images in a folder, mark the "Change image" field and then select how often the image should be changed, e.g every hour. The images are displayed in the order they appear in the folder. However, you can also choose a random order.

To use a picture from the Photos app, select the picture in the app, then click the Share button

on the Photos toolbar. Then select "Set as desktop background".

a picture from the web can serve the purpose of desktop picture. Double click the image in the browser window and choose "Use image as desktop background".

USE YOUR INTERNET ACCOUNT ON MAC

You can use Exchange, Google, and Yahoo! accounts, as well as other internet accounts, in Mac apps. To do this, you need to add these accounts to your Mac.

You can add Internet accounts and manage account settings in the "Internet Accounts" system settings. You can also add internet accounts in some of the apps that use them.

An iCloud account that you add in the "iCloud" area of the "Apple ID" system preference is also displayed in the "Internet accounts" system preference. You can alter the settings in both places.

Add an account from an app

You can add accounts from the Mail, Contacts, and Calendar apps. Accounts that you add in the apps are displayed in the "Internet accounts" system settings.

- In an app on your Mac, click on the app's menu and select "Add Account".
  Select in the app "Mail" . "Mail"> "Add Account".

- Select the provider of the account and follow the instructions on the screen.

  If you want to add a provider account (for example, an email or calendar account for your company or school) that is not on the list, click on "Other [type] account", and then touch "Continue" after which the required account settings should be entered. If you don't know the account settings, ask the provider.

Add an account in the system settings "Internet accounts"

In order to be able to add an account in the "Internet accounts" system setting, you have to set it up in advance on the website of your provider.

- on MacTap "Apple" > "System settings" and touch "Internet accounts".
- Click on an account provider.

  If you do not yet have an account from a certain provider (e.g. for Yahoo!), you first have to create one on the website of the respective provider.

If you want to add a provider account (for example an email or calendar account for your company or school) that is not on the list, tap "Add Another Account", then touch the type of account you have, after whichthe required account settings should be entered. If you don't know the type of account or the account settings, ask the provider.

- Enter the account name, password, and any other information you need.
- In the case of an account that supports various functions, select the functions you want to use from the list on the right.

Change account functions and detailed information

on MacTap "Apple" > "System settings" and tap "Internet accounts".

Select an account in the list on the left and do one of the following:

Activate or deactivate functions: Activate the functions you want to use and deactivate the functions you do not want to use.

Change detailed information of the account: Click in the area of the selected account on the right on "Details". For some accounts, details such as account name, description, and other information are displayed on the right. In this instance the "Details" button is not usable.

Stop using an account

- on Mac touch "Apple" > "System settings" and tap "Internet accounts".
- Select the account that you no longer want to use, and do one of the following:
  - i. Remove account and switch off its functions: Click on the "Remove" button

    .

    If you have iCloud Keychain set up on your Mac , when you remove an account (except for your primary iCloud account), you will be asked if you want to remove the account from your other Mac computers that use iCloud Keychain, or if only all functions of the respective account should be switched off on this Mac.

ii. Deactivate special function: Deactivate the corresponding option.

ATTENTION: If you delete an account or deactivate individual functions of an account, there is a possibility that data stored in your apps will be removed. The data may be restored if you reactivate the feature or add the account again.

USE A SCREEN SAVER ON YOUR MAC

You can use a screen saver to hide your desk when you're away from your Mac for a while or when you need more privacy.

- on MacTap "Apple" > "System Preferences", touch "Desktop & Screensaver" and then on "Screensaver".
- Click on a screen saver on the left and set the options for it on the right.The options available depend on the screen saver you selected.

i.   Source: Click the pop-up menu, then choose the images you want to appear in the screen saver. You can use pictures built into macOS or choose pictures from your photo library or from another folder.

ii.   The screen saver is displayed in the preview area. It will take a moment for your selection to preview.

iii. Random order of slides: Check this box to display the images in a random order instead of the order in the source.

iv.   Screensaver Options: Click this button to set the color, speed, and other options.

- Determine when the screen saver should start.

i.   Start up after: Click the pop-up menu and choose how long you want your Mac to wait before starting the screen saver.

ii.   Show with clock: Check this box to display the time in the screensaver.

iii. Use random screensaver: Check this box to have the macOS screen saver selected.

iv.   Active corners: Click this button to set a shortcut that you can use to start the screensaver immediately at any time.

Press any key, touch the trackpad or move the mouse, To exit the screen saver and return to the desktop.

CHANGE YOUR PICTURE OR ANYONE ELSE'S PICTURE IN APPS ON MAC

You can change the picture that appears to you and others in apps like Mail or Messages on your Mac.

ATTENTION: On your Mac, you can also change the image on the login screen that appears next to your name or someone else's name in the login window.

Images in the "Mail" app

Depending on the pictures available in the Contacts app, Mail can display a picture for you and for people who send you email. The pictures are only shown to you. They will not be included in your email.

Images in the "Messages" app

The pictures of you and your friends displayed in the Messages app may vary:

- When you and your friends share photos or memoji (using macOS Big Sur), they will see your shared picture and you will see their shared pictures.
- If you and your friends aren't sharing photos or memoji (with macOS Big Sur), or if your friends are using macOS 10.15 (or earlier), they'll see the picture they have of you in their Contacts app, and you'll see the picture that you have from them in your app "Contacts".

Pictures in the "Contacts" app

Your photos can be added to your contact card and add pictures from your contacts to their cards. The images you choose are only visible to you and not to your contacts.

SET UP USERS, GUESTS, AND GROUPS FOR THE MAC

If you have more than one person using your Mac, you should set up a separate account for each of these people so that each user can set their own preferences and options without affecting the other users. You can permitinfrequent users to sign in as a guest without havingaccess to other users' files or settings. It is also possible to create groups. You must be an administrator on your Mac to perform these tasks .

add user

- on Mac Tap "Apple" > "System Settings" and tap "Users & Groups".
  When the lock is closed on the lower left, click the lock to unlock System Preferences.
- Tap "Add" under the user list.
- Click the New Account pop-up menu and choose the type of user you want.
  i. Administrator: An administrator has the rights to add and manage other users, install apps and change settings. The user you created when you first set up your Mac is automatically configured as an administrator. You can configure multiple administrators on your Mac. You can create

new administrator accounts and downgrade an administrator to a standard user. It is not recommended to enable automatic login for an administrator. If this happens, someone could simply restart your Mac to gain administrative access to your Mac. To protect your computer, you should not disclose administrator names and passwords.

ii. Standard: Standard users are set up by an administrator. It is possible for Standard users to install apps and modify their own settings. However, you cannot add other users or change other users' settings.

iii. Share only: Share only users can remotely access shared files. However, they will not be able to log on to the computer or change any settings on the computer. If you want the user to have access to your shared files or a split screen, you may need to change settings in the File Sharing, Screen Sharing, or Remote Management sections of the Sharing preferences.

For more information on the options for each type of user, click the Help button in the lower left corner of the dialog box

- the full name of the new user should be entered. The name of theaccount isautomatically generated. If you are desirous of using a distinct account name, enter it now as it cannot be altered later.
- Enter a password for the user and enter the same password again to confirm. Enter a memory aid to help the user remember the password.
- Click on "Create User".
- Additionally, depending on the type of user you are creating, you can do any of the following:
  i. Select "The user can manage this computer" if the account should be set up as an administrator account.
  ii. For an administrator, select "User can reset their password using their Apple ID".

iii. In the "Shares" system preferences, determine whether the user has access to your files and your screen.

If your Mac has Touch ID, a new user can add a fingerprint after signing in to your Mac. The user can then use Touch ID to unlock the Mac and password-protected items, and to use their Apple ID to purchase items in the iTunes Store, App Store, and Apple Books.

Create a group

A group enables several users to use the same access rights. For example, you can give a group specific access rights to a folder or file. Then all group members can use this access. It is also possible to assign specific access rights to each of your shared folders to a group.

- on Mac touch "Apple"> "System Settings" and tap "Users & Groups".

    When the lock 🔒 is closed on the lower left, click the lock to unlock System Preferences .

- Tap "Add" ┬ under the user list.
- Tap the "New Account" pop-up menu and select "Group".
- Write a name for the group and touch "Create group".
- Select each user and group that you want to add to the new group.

In the "Shares" system settings, determine whether group members have access to your files and your screen .

Convert standard user to administrator

- on your Mactouch "Apple" > "System Settings" and tap "Users & Groups".

  When the lock 🔒is closed on the lower left , click the lock to unlock System Preferences .

- Select a standard user or a managed user in the user list and select "The user is allowed to manage this computer".

Allow occasional users to log in as a guest

You can allow other people to temporarily use your Mac as guest users without having to add them as individual users.

- Guests do not need a password to log in.
- Guests cannot make changes to user or computer settings.
- Guests cannot log in from another computer if remote logon is enabled in the "Shares" system preference.

Files created by a guest are stored in a temporary folder, which is deleted and all its contents are deleted when the guest logs off.

When you log in as a guest user, the "Search" function is available so that you can search for your lost Mac. You can track your Mac immediately someone finds your Mac, sign in as a guest, and access the Internetusing Safari.

Note: When File Vault is enabled, guests can access Safari, but they cannot access your encrypted volumes or create files.

- on Mactouch "Apple" > "System Settings" then tap "Users & Groups".

  When the lock is closed on the lower left, click the lock to unlock System Preferences.
- from the list of userschoose "Guest User".
- Touch "Allow guests to logonto this computer".
- If necessary, check the "Restrict adult content" checkbox to prevent guest users from accessing websites with adult content.
- Check the "Allow guests access to shared folders" checkbox if you want to allow guests to access your shared folders from another computer on the network.

Customize the login process

As an administrator, you can control the appearance of the login screen that all other users see.

- on the Mac Select "Apple" > "System settings". Handpick "Users & Groups" and on "Login Options".

- When the lock is closed on the lower left, click the lock to unlock System Preferences.

- Click on the "Automatic login" pop-up menu and select a user or, alternatively, the entry "Off".

- If you select a user, they'll be logged in automatically every time the Mac starts up. If you select "Off", the Mac opens a login window when it starts, showing all users. You will be automatically signed in the next time you restart your Mac

- Note: The automatic login implies that any user can gain immediate access to your Mac by simply restarting the device. For this reason, if you enable automatic login, it is important to ensure that you are not automatically logged into your Mac as an administrator. When FileVault is enabled, automatic login is automatically disabled.

- Select the options you want. Click on a question on the button ? "Help", to display detailed information.

If you want to give a new user access to your shared files or a split screen, you may need to change settings in the File Sharing, Screen Sharing, or Remote Management sections of the Sharing preferences.

To open the "Shares" setting, select "Apple"> "System Settings" and click on "Shares".

OPTIMIZE YOUR SCREEN DISPLAY ON YOUR MAC

If you have trouble seeing or recognizing certain objects on the screen while working on your Mac, follow these suggestions.

Change the appearance of the desk

- Reduce the transparency of the desk: Select "Apple"> "System settings". Click Accessibility, click Display, and choose Reduce Transparency. The transparent areas of the desk and the app window are highlighted in gray.

- Choose a simpler wallpaper : Choose Apple menu> System Preferences, click Desktop & Screensavers, click Desktop, then browse the folders with the images on the left and choose a simpler or solid background on the right.

- Make edges darker: select Apple menu> System Preferences, tap Accessibility, touch Display, then tap Increase Contrast. macOS then automatically reduces the transparency and makes the borders of buttons, fields and other objects on the screen more visible.

- Use a dark appearance: select Apple menu> System Preferences, tap General, then touch the Dark appearance. You can modify the accent and selection colors.

- Invert colors: Choose Apple menu> System Preferences. Click Accessibility, click Display, click Display, and choose Invert Colors. When you turn on Night Shift, the Invert Colors option is automatically turned off.

- See colors better at night: Use Night Shift to make the colors on the screen warmer.

- Differentiate or tone down colors: apply color filters or colorize the entire screen.

- To enlarge the pointer: Choose Apple menu> System Preferences, click Accessibility, click Display, click Pointer, then drag the pointer size slider to the right until the size you want.

Tip: If you don't know where the pointer is on the screen, you can quickly move your finger on the trackpad or the mouse. The pointer will then temporarily zoom in so you can see it. To turn off this feature, choose Apple> System Preferences. Click Accessibility, click Display, click Cursor, and then deselect the checkbox for "Shake the mouse pointer to find it."

Enlarge text

- Enlarge email text in Mail: Choose Mail> Preferences in Mail, click Font & Color, click Choose next to Email Fonts, and choose a font size in the Fonts window out.

- Make the text of a message bigger: Choose Messages> Preferences, click General, then drag the Text Size slider to the right.

- Enlarging text in other apps: In many apps you can adjust the font size with the key combinations "Command ($\mathcal{H}$) -Plus (+)" or "Command ($\mathcal{H}$) -minus (-)". If these commands don't work, check the app's settings.

Enlarge symbols and other objects

- Enlarging symbols and symbol text on the desktop: Hold down the "ctrl" key while clicking on the desktop, select "Show display options" and move the slider for the symbol size to the right. Choose the Text Size pop-up menu, then select a text size.

- Make icons and text bigger in the Finder: Select an item in the Finder, then choose View> Show View Options. The representation used determines how you can enlarge the text.

  i. Symbol display: Move the "Symbol size" slider to the right. Touch the Text Size pop-up menu, then hand pick a text size.

ii. List display: Select a higher value for the symbol size to the right of " Symbol size ". Touch the Text Size pop-up menu, then select a text size.

iii. Column display : Click the Text Size pop-up menu and choose a text size. You cannot change the icon size.

iv. Gallery display: Select the highest value for the miniature size. You cannot choose a text size.

- Enlarge items in the sidebar in Finder and Mail: Choose Apple > "System settings" and click on "General". Then choose Large from the Sidebar Icon Size pop-up menu.

Use zoom

- To zoom in on the screen: Select "Apple" > "System Settings" and click on "Accessibility" and then on "Zoom". You can zoom in on the entire screen or just part of the screen.

i. When Use Keyboard Shortcuts to Zoom is on, you can zoom in (press Option-Command-Equals Sign), zoom out (press

Option-Command-Minus Sign), or quickly switch between the two settings (press Option-Command-8 ").

ii. When Zoom In: Scroll Gesture With These Special Keys is selected, you can zoom in by holding down the Control key (or another special key) and sliding two fingers up on the trackpad.

- To zoom in on an item under the mouse pointer: Choose Apple menu> System Preferences, then click Accessibility. Then tap "Zoom" and touch "Enable floating text".

- To zoom in on web pages: In Safari, choose View > Zoom In or press Command (⌘) -Plus (+). You can click "Zoom In" repeatedly or press Command (⌘) -Plus (+) to increase the magnification. If you only want to enlarge the text and not the images, select Zoom To Text Only.

- Zoom in on PDF files, images and websites: You can zoom in and out with a simple gesture, provided your mouse or trackpad supports it. To do this, choose Apple menu> System Preferences, click Mouse> Point And Click, or Trackpad> Scroll And Zoom, then choose Smart Zoom. You can then zoom in and in by double-tapping - on the mouse, by double-tapping with one finger, on the trackpad, by double-tapping with two fingers.

USE ACCESSIBILITY ON MAC

Accessibility features are standard on every Mac. If you have trouble seeing or hearing, or if your physical mobility is restricted, you will find numerous functions in macOS that allow you to work in alternative ways and make the Mac easier to use.

Use the built-in VoiceOver screen reader

VoiceOver is the built-in text-to-speech feature on your Mac that reads aloud what is on screen. You can also have the content of documents, websites and windows read out to you. VoiceOver lets you control your Mac using the keyboard or trackpad gestures, or you can connect an updateable Braille display for use with VoiceOver. to customize VoiceOveremploy the VoiceOver utility.

Increasing the volume of the content on the page

- You can use the mouse or trackpad to zoom in and zoom in on all or part of the screen. If you're using a second screen with your Mac, you can select the screen to zoom in or zoom in on both screens.
- You can use floating text to enlarge the objects under the mouse cursor - text, fields, menu items, buttons, and more - and display them in high resolution in a separate window.

Reduce movement on the screen

If you're having trouble with movement on the Mac screen, you can set an option to reduce movement when using certain features (like Spaces, Notification Center, and Dock).

Using physical keyboard or possibly an on-screen keyboard

You can use options to enable one-touch or key delay to make it easier for you to press keys on a physical keyboard. You can also bypass the need for a physical keyboard altogether and use the on-screen accessibility keyboard instead .

Control pointer and mouse actions using alternative methods

- When you turn on mouse operation, you can control the pointer with the keyboard or the numeric keypad.
- When alternate pointer actions is activated, you can carry out mouse actions (such as drag-and-drop actionor a left-click) with keyboard shortcuts, switches, or facial expressions (such as smiling or opening your mouth).
- When you turn on the head pointer, you can move the pointer based on the movement of your face or head as detected by the camera built into or attached to the Mac.

Use voice control and speech output

- With voice control, you can use spoken commands to open apps, select menu items, and more. macOS offers a standard selection of commands and also allows you to create your own commands.

- You can set up your Mac to read text in dialog boxes and warning messages aloud, and to notify you when user action is required (for example, when you receive an invitation through the Messages app).

Change how the keyboard, mouse, and trackpad work

You can set various options on your Mac to customize how the keyboard, mouse, and trackpad work. For example, you can vary the speed at which the pointer moves across the screen when you swipe your finger on the trackpad. Select "Apple" to set these options > "System Preferences" and click on "Keyboard", "Mouse" or "Trackpad".

Control your Mac with auxiliary devices

- Switch controls let you enter text with one or more customizable tools, interact with objects on the screen, and control your Mac. The switch control scans an area of the screen or the user interface until a switch is triggered to select an object or perform an action.

- With the Accessibility Keyboard , you can use Dwell Control with a controller to control the pointer so you can easily enter text, interact with onscreen objects, and control your Mac. With the dwell control you can dwell on a control element for a specified period of time in order to carry out a mouse action.

You   can use the Accessibility   Shortcut   Panel to quickly turn some accessibility features on and off.

RUNNING WINDOWS ON YOUR MAC

You can use Boot Camp software to install and use Windows on your Intel-based Mac.

Boot Camp Assistant will help you set up a Windows partition on the hard drive of your Mac computer and then install your Windows software.

After installing Windows and the Boot Camp drivers, you can either start your Mac in Windows or macOS.

CREATE YOUR OWN MEMOJI IN MESSAGES ON MAC

Create a personalized memoji that matches your personality in macOS Big Sur. You can then send Memoji stickers to express your current mood in the messages.

- Select any conversation in the Messages app on your Mac.
- In the lower-left corner of the window, next to the field, click the Apps 🍎 button, then select the Memoji Stickers 😀 button.
- Click the Add ✛ button, then follow the instructions that appear to customize your Memoji - from skin color to headwear.
- Click on "Done".

BURN CDS AND DVDS ON MAC

If your Mac has a built-in optical drive or if you connect an external DVD drive (such as an Apple USB SuperDrive), you can burn files to CDs or DVDs to share your files with friends, transfer them between computers, or to Make backup copies of your files. DVDs / CDs that burned with your Mac can as well be used on Windows computers and on other kinds of computers.

- Put in a blank disc into your optical drive.
  If a dialog box appears, click the pop-up menu, then choose Open Finder. Check the box "Use this action as default" if you want the Finder to open every time you insert a blank CD / DVD. The CD / DVD will appear on your desk.

- Open the CD / DVD window by double-clicking the CD / DVD icon and dragging the files and folders you want to burn to the CD / DVD into the window.
  Alias files of the selected files are placed in the CD / DVD window . The original files are neither moved nor deleted.
  Note: If you want to burn the same files onto multiple CDs or DVDs, use a burn folder .

- Arrange and rename the files.
  When burning, the objects on the CD / DVD are given the same name and position as in the CD

/ DVD window. After burning the CD / DVD, you can no longer change the objects.

- Choose File> Burn [disc name], then follow the instructions that appear.

The files referenced by the alias files are burned onto the CD / DVD. If you add folders to the CD / DVD that contain aliases, the files that the aliases point to are also burned onto the CD / DVD.

ATTENTION: If you eject the CD / DVD without burning any data on it, a burn folder with the selected items will be created and placed on your desktop. To stop the burn process, click the "Burn" icon next to the folder in the Finder sidebar or hold down the "Control" key and click the appropriate DVD / CD and tap "Burn DVD /CD" from context menu.

To burn an image file (file with the extension .dmg) to a storage medium, while holding down the "ctrl" key, click on the image file, select

" Burn [image name] to DVD / CD " in the context menu and adhere to other instructions.

ATTENTION: To delete the contents of a rewritable storage medium, hold down the "Control" key and click on the CD or DVD drive in the sidebar of the Finder and select the option to delete the rewritable storage medium from the context menu.

CHAPTER SIX

PODCAST

SIGN IN TO THE PODCASTS APP ON THE MAC: To store and listen to podcasts sign in with your Apple ID .

- With the Podcasts app on your device, select Account> Sign In.

   If you're already signed in to the Music app or the Apple TV app, you're automatically signed in to the Podcasts app too.

- Perform one of the following:

Sign in with your Apple ID: Enter your Apple ID Apple ID and your password and click on "Next".

Create an Apple ID: Click "Create Apple ID" and follow the instructions that appear.

To sign out, touch the "Apple" menu > "System Preferences" and select "Apple ID". Then tap "Overview" and on "sign out".

SEARCH FOR PODCAST ON MAC

Find free podcasts in many categories such as science, news, comedy and more and play them - similar to radio or TV shows. You can subscribe to your favorite shows and listen to new episodes right after they're released. You can also download episodes to your library and listen to them when you are not connected to the Internet.

ATTENTION: If you want to quickly find different shows, click on "Discover" in the sidebar on the left to display shows that are marked as "Highlights", "New" and "Noteworthy". You can search by categories or curated collections.

You can search podcasts by title, subject, guest, host, and more. You can search all available podcasts or just those already in your library.

- In the Podcasts app on your Mac, click the search box in the upper-left corner of the Podcasts window (or press Command-F), then do one of the following:

i.   Search all podcasts: Enter what you are looking for, click on "All Podcasts" on the right and select a suggestion or press Return.

ii. Search your media library: Enter what you are looking for, click on "Your media library" on the right and select a suggestion or press Return.

- In the search findings, do any of the following:

i.   Play a show or episode : Hold the pointer over a show or episode, then click the play

⊙ button.

ii. View details about the program or episode: Click on the title link in the program area. In the episode section, click the title link next to the relevant episode.

iii. Subscribe to a program : Hold the pointer over a program, click the "More" button

● ● ●

and select "Subscribe".

iv.   Show more results : If more results match the search criteria, click "Show all" to the right of "Programs" or "Episodes".

Ask Siri: For instance you can say, "What kind of podcast is this?".

Note: Some podcasts may contain material intended for an adult audience, such as content in open language or adult topics and situations.

LISTEN TO PODCASTS ON MAC

Podcasts are free audio broadcasts that you can stream and play on your Mac. You can listen to individual podcast episodes or subscribe to a show so that new episodes are automatically loaded into your library as soon as they are available.

Your subscriptions, channels, and the current playback position will be synced with the Podcasts app on all of your devices when you sign in with the same Apple ID .

- In the Podcasts app on your Mac, click Listen Now (or an item) in the sidebar.

- Place the pointer over the show or episode you would like to play, then tap the play button .

When the episode starts playing, the playback controls appear at the top of the Podcasts window.

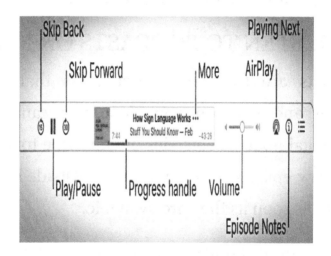

- Perform one of the following with the playback controls:

i.   Play or pause: tap the Play ▶ button or

Pause ⏸ button (you can also make use of
the playback controls in the Touch Bar)
You can also press the spacebar to play,
pause, and resume a program.

ii.   (15) : Advance or go back Click on the

button (15) "spring back", jump back (in
15-second increments) in the sequence, or

the button (30) "prominence" (in 30-
second increments) to protrude (or
possiblyemploy the playback controls in
the Touch Bar).
Tip: You can set the time that an episode
jumps forward or backward.

iii.   Rewind or fast forward: Click on a point
in the status bar to jump directly there, or
move the handle left to rewind or right to

fast forward (you can also makeuse of the playback controls in the Touch Bar).

iv. Change the playback tempo :Choose Control> Playback Tempo, then choose a tempo.

v. Adjust volume: Drag the volume slider right or left to increase or decrease the volume (or possiblyemploy the playback controls in the Touch Bar).

vi. Speaker Select: Click on the button "AirPlay" ⧉, the speaker you want to use.

vii. Manage an episode (for example, copy the link, share the episode, or go to the detail page): Hold the pointer over an episode that's currently playing, click the More button ●, and choose an option.

viii. Read the episode description: Click the Episodes button ⓘ.

Ask Siri: For example, say:

"Jump 3 minutes forward"

"Continue with the last podcast"

In Notification Center, you can see which episode is on and even what's next on the list. Add the Up Next Podcasts widget to quickly resume playback.

LISTEN TO PODCASTS ON ALL OF YOUR DEVICES

You can see your subscriptions, stations, and the current playback position for your podcasts on your Mac, iPhone, iPad, and iPod touch if you're signed in with the same Apple ID on all devices.

On your Mac: In the Podcasts app, choose Podcasts> Preferences, then click Advanced. Ensurethe "Sync subscriptions across devices"option is activated.

On your, iPod touch,iPad,iPhone: select Settings> Podcasts, then enable Sync Podcasts.

If you have an iPod classic, iPod nano, or iPod shuffle, you'll need to sync your device with your Mac in order to add podcasts and other content to it.

SUBSCRIBE OR UNSUBSCRIBE TO PODCASTS ON MAC

You can subscribe to podcasts you like (for free) and automatically download new episodes as they become available. If you are no longer interested in a podcast, unsubscribe from the program in question.

Subscribe to the podcast

- Get your app in the "podcasts" on the Mac to search for podcasts or click on an object in "Apple Podcasts" in the left sidebar.
- Select a show to view its information page, then click the Subscribe button + Subscribe .

You can automatically load new or unplayed episodes.

Attention: You can also subscribe to a podcast via its URL. Choose File> Add A Show Via URL, enter the URL of the RSS feed, then click Subscribe. Usually the URL is on the podcast website.

End podcast subscription

In the Podcasts app on your Mac, click Broadcasts in the sidebar on the left.

Hold the pointer over a program, click the "More" buttonand select "End subscription".

USE THE NEXT TRACK LIST IN THE PODCASTS APP ON MAC

While playing podcasts, you can use the Next Track List to view episodes (or chapters of an episode) and change the order in which they play.

Using the Next Track List

- In the Podcasts app on your Mac, click an option in the sidebar.
  Hover over a show you're subscribed to or an episode, click the More ⋯ button,then choose Next Track or Last Track.
- The show or episode is added to the top of the "Next Track" list when you select "Next Track". It appears at the bottom of the list when you select "Last Track".

- In the upper-right corner of the Podcasts window, click the Next Track button $\equiv$, then do one of the following:

  i. Play an episode (or chapters in a episode) in the list: Click on the episode or chapter.

      Attention: The episodes of some podcasts are divided into chapters. This allows you to quickly jump to a specific point in the sequence.

  ii. To change the order of episodes that were manually added to the list: move episodes with the Reorder button $\equiv$.

The Next Track list appears until you click the button $\equiv$ again to close the list.

Ask Siri: For example, say:

"Play the next episode"

Remove episode from the "Next Track" list

- In the Podcasts app on your Mac, do one of the following to remove an episode from the Next Track list:

i. Touch the Next Track button ≡ in the upper right of the Podcasts window, swipe left on the episode in the list with two fingers (if you have a trackpad or magic mouse), then click Remove.

ii. Click on "Follow" in the sidebar under "Media", search for the episode you want to remove, click the "More" button next to the episode and then select " Mark as played".

ADD, DOWNLOAD, AND REMOVE PODCAST EPISODES ON MAC

You can add episodes to your library and then download selected episodes so you can play them even if you don't have an internet connection - even if you haven't subscribed to the podcast.

Add or load a single episode

- Get your app in the "podcasts" on the Mac to search for podcasts or click on an object in "Apple Podcasts" in the left sidebar.

- To add an episode to your library, move the pointer over the episode, then do one of the following:

    i.   Click the Add button $+$.

    ii. Tap the "More" button $\cdots$ and choose "Add to Library".

    ATTENTION: it may be necessary to select a show in other to view its episodes.

- To load the episode into your library, move the pointer over the episode, then performany of the following:

    i.   Click the "Load" button ⛅.

    ii. Tap the "More" button $\cdots$ and then handpick " Load episode".

Enable automatic downloads

You can automatically download new or unplayed episodes of a subscribed podcast.

- In the Podcasts app on Mac, select Podcasts> Preferences, then tap General.

- Click the Auto Load Episodes pop-up menu, then choose the appropriate option to automatically load new or unplayed episodes.

Remove a single episode

- In the Podcasts app on your Mac, click Follow in the sidebar on the left under Library, then do the following to remove an individual episode:

  i. Swipe left over the episode with two fingers (if you're using a trackpad or magic mouse), then click Delete to remove the episode from your computer.

  ii. Control-click the episode you want to delete, click Remove, and then choose Delete from Library (to remove the episode only from your library) or Remove Download (to remove the episode from your computer Clear).

ATTENTION: You can delete more than one episode at a time. To select multiple adjacent sequences, click the first object you want to select, hold the Shift key, then click the last object. To select multiple non-contiguous episodes, Command-click the episodes of interest.You can automatically delete episodes you've already listened to.

If you have an iPod classic, iPod nano, or iPod shuffle, you'll need to sync your device with your Mac in order to add podcasts and other content to it.

CREATE AND MANAGE PODCAST STATIONS ON MAC

You can create stations (previously named in iTunes playlists) with subscribed podcasts, for example to combine all podcasts on personal finance into one station. You can then play the podcasts in your station in any order. As soon as new episodes are available, the channels are automatically updated with them.

This is the symbol of a station, which is displayed next to the station.

Create and edit podcast stations

- In the Podcasts app on Mac, tap File > New Station.

- Enter a name for the station and click on "Save".
- Update one of the following settings for the transmitter:
    i. Station: Enter a different station name if necessary.
    ii. Playback: Select the order in which the podcasts are played in the station.
    iii. Group by podcast: Check this box if you want the station to be organized by podcast.
    iv. Episodes: Select which episodes should be included in the broadcaster.
    v. Media Type: Specify whether to include audio only podcasts, video only podcasts, or podcasts of both types.
    vi. Only unplayed episodes : Check this box to include episodes that have not yet been played.
- Click on "Select Podcasts" and select the programs that should be included in the station. Or tap "Include All Podcasts" and then touch "OK".

- Click on "OK".

The station is displayed in the "Station" area under the media library.

To edit the station, click on the "More" button ●●● in the upper right corner then select "Settings".

Play podcast stations

- In the Podcasts app on Mac, tap a station in the sidebar.
- Perform one of the following:
  i. Hold the pointer over the show or episode that you want to play, then click the Play ▶ button.

  ii. Click the More ●●● button in the upper right corner, then select Play.

Delete podcast stations

- In the Podcasts app on your Mac, touch a station in the sidebar.

- Click on the "More" button • • • in the upper right corner and then select "Delete channels".

The channels are synced on all devices that are signed in with the same Apple ID and that sync is turned on.

READ OR WRITE REVIEWS IN THE PODCASTS APP ON YOUR MAC

You can read the reviews of other listeners for a podcast and write a review yourself.

- In the Podcasts app on your Mac, click Broadcasts in the sidebar on the left.
- Select a show to view its information page, then scroll down to the Ratings & Reviews section.
- Perform one of the following:
  i. Read reviews: Click on the button "Forward" ❯ or "Back" button ❮, to read individual reviews, or click on "View All" to the overall rating of the program and more reviews from listeners indicate.

ii. Write your own review: Click on "Write a review" and enter your review. Then click on "Save".

After you've saved it, you can edit the review. To perform this, tap "Write a review", make appropriate changes and then touch "Save".

ATTENTION: You can also rate a show on a scale from one to five stars to show how you liked the show. Just hold the pointer over the stars and click or move the pointer to increase or decrease the number of stars.

CHOOSE YOUR PODCAST AND EPISODE PREFERENCES ON MAC

After you locate podcasts you prefer, you can subscribe to them , share them with friends.

Select podcast settings

- In your Podcasts app on Mac, tap Broadcasts in the sidebar on the left.

- Select a program to view its information page. Touch the "More" ••• button and then on "Settings".
- Do one of the following:

   i. Subscribe to a broadcast or end a subscription: Activate or deactivate the "Subscribe" option.

  ii. Select sequence of episodes for playback: Either play the episodes in sequence or always have the most recent episode played first.

 iii. Choose which episodes you want to keep. Click "Keep Only The Latest Episodes", then scroll down to choose how many of the unplayed episodes to keep.

 iv. Customize settings: Click on "My Settings" then scroll down to specify which episodes should be loaded and saved and how often should be updated.

Share or delete podcasts, add to Next Track List, and more

- In the Podcasts app on your Mac, touch Broadcasts in the sidebar on the left.

- Select a program to view its information page. Tap the More ••• button, then performany of the following:

i. Remove podcast from the library: Select "Delete from library".

   This action also deletes all episodes.

   Note: If you only want to remove one episode, select "Episodes" in the sidebar on the left, hold down the "ctrl" key and click on the episode and then select "Remove".

ii. To add a podcast to the "Next Track" list: Select "Next Track".

   Tap "Play last" to shift the show down in the list. You can manually change the order in the "Next Track" list ≣ by moving the episodes with the " Reorder " button.

iii. Copy link: Select "Copy link".

The link is copied to the clipboard. then You can paste the link intoother document. When you click the link, the show will open in the Podcasts app.

iv.   Share a podcast: Choose Share Show, then share it via email, text message, or as a shared note, or use AirDrop to send it to someone nearby.

To add an episode to the media library from the show's information page, click on "View All Episodes" (you may have to scroll to see this link) and then click the "Add" button next to an episode. To download the episode so you can play it when you don't have an internet connection, click the Load button ⬇.

Select settings for a sequence

- In the Podcasts app on your Mac, click Follow in the sidebar on the left.

- Hold the pointer over a sequence, click the More ••• button, and do any of the following:

i. Load episode: Select the "Load episode" option for episodes that you have added to your library.

ii. Remove downloaded episode from your computer: Select "Remove".

Note: If the episode is not loaded, you can select the option "Delete from library" and remove the episode from your library.

iii. Save episode: Select "Save episode".

iv. Mark episode as played or unplayed:Select "Mark as played" or "Mark as unplayed".

If you mark an episode as unplayed, it will remain in the "Next Track" list and can be played again.

v. To add a sequence to the "Next Track" list: Select "Next Track".

Select "Play Recently" to move the episode down the list.

vi. Copy link: Select "Copy link".

The link is copied to the clipboard. thenYou can paste the link into other document. When you click the link, the show will open in the Podcasts app.

vii. Share an episode: Select Share an episode, then share it via email, text message, or as a shared note, or use AirDrop to send it to someone nearby.

viii. Show information   page: Select   "To broadcast".

MANAGE EPISODE NOTIFICATIONS IN THE PODCASTS APP ON MAC

You can be notified when a new episode of a program you have subscribed to is available.

- In the Podcasts app on Mac, tap Podcasts> Notifications.
- To receive notifications for a subscribed program (or to deactivate it), activate or deactivate the switch with one click.
- Click on "OK".

RESTRICT ACCESS TO PODCASTS WITH INAPPROPRIATE CONTENT ON MAC

You can prevent people using your Mac from accessing adult podcasts.

- Choose "Apple" menu on Mac > "System Settings" and touch "Screen Time".
- Tap "Content & Privacy" in the sidebar.
- If the option "Content & Privacy" is deactivated, click on "Activate".
- Performany of the following:
  i. Deactivate the app from an iOS or iPadOS device: Click on "Apps" and deactivate "Podcasts".
  ii. Exclude podcasts with offensive content: Click on "Stores" and deactivate "Offensive music, podcasts & news"

CHAPTER SEVEN

DEVICE PROTECTION

PROTECT YOUR MAC COMPUTER FROM MALWARE

macOS has many features to help protect your Mac and personal data from malware. Malware is often spread by inserting it into an unsuspicious app.

You can reduce the risk by only using software from reliable sources. You can use the preferences in Security Preferences to specify the sources of software that can be installed on your Mac.

- Choose "Apple" on Mac > "System Settings" and tap "Security" and then on "General".

  When the lock is closed in the lower left, click the lock to unlock System Preferences.

- Choose the sources from which software can be installed:

i. App Store: Only apps from the Mac App Store are allowed. This setting offers the greatest security. All developers who want to offer their apps in the Mac App Store are identified and verified by Apple, and every app is checked before it is accepted. macOS checks an app before opening it for the first time to ensure that no modifications have been made to it since the app was published by the developer. If problems arise with an app, Apple will remove the app in question from the Mac App Store.

ii. App Store and Verified Developers: Only apps from the Mac App Store or from developers who have been verified by Apple are allowed. Verified developers are registered with Apple and can, if desired, upload their apps to Apple for a security check. If there are problems with an app, Apple can revoke its authorization and approval. macOS checks an app before opening it for the first time to ensure that no modifications have been made to it since the app was published by the developer.

In addition to apps, other file types can also be unsafe. Scripts, web archives, and Java archives can potentially damage your system. Of course, not all such files are unsafe, but you should be careful when opening such loaded files. A warning will appear the first time you try to open these files.

PROTECT YOUR PRIVACY ON MAC

Privacy and the protection of personal data are important issues when apps exchange information over the Internet. macOS provides security-related functions with which you can strengthen the protection of your personal data and determine the extent to which information about you and your Mac is made available on the Internet.

Use screen time

With Screen Time, you can monitor your children's use of the computer and prevent access to certain websites. For

Choose "Apple" > "System Settings" and touch "Screen Time".

Use Safari features to protect your privacy

Safari offers many features to protect your privacy on the Internet. For example, you can browse privately so that Safari doesn't record the websites you visit and the items you load. In addition, you can pop-up window blocking , sites prevent cookies from being stored on your Mac and more.

Control the amount of personal information published via apps

With the help of location services, apps (e.g. web browsers) can collect and use information about your current location. You can turn off location services entirely. But you can also specifically select the apps that should be able to access your location information.

Some apps collect and use information from your contacts, photos, calendars, and reminders. Some apps use your Mac's microphone and camera.

Decide wisely about sharing analytics data

You can help Apple to further improve the quality and performance of its products and services. For this purpose, macOS can automatically collect analysis data about your Mac and transmit it to Apple for further analysis. The information is only transferred to Apple anonymously and with your consent.

You can specify whether analysis data should be sent to Apple in the "Privacy" area of the "Security" system setting.

Choose "Apple" > "System Settings", tap "Security", on "Privacy" and then handpick "Analysis & Improvements".

Set up a firewall

You can set up a firewall to block unwanted communication with your Mac from the network and thus help protect your privacy. If the firewall is activated, you can also use what is known as "stealth mode", in which your Mac cannot be seen by other participants on the Internet.

To set up and adapt your firewall, use the "Firewall" section of the "Security" system setting.

Choose "Apple" > "System settings" and tap "Security" and then on "Firewall".

USE SIGN IN WITH APPLE ON MAC

The "Sign in with Apple" option is an easy and secure way to sign in to apps and websites. It uses your Apple ID to securely create an account for an app or website. This eliminates the need to fill out a form, verify your email address or choose a new password. Each registration process is thus significantly simplified.

Creating an account for a website anor app

- When your Mac asks if you want to create an account for an app or website, click the Sign In With Apple or Continue With Apple button (if available).
- Follow the instructions on the screen, taking note of the following:
  i. Click on the "Name" field and enter a different name if you do not want to use your real name.
  ii. If your Apple ID has multiple email addresses associated with it in Apple ID settings, select the email address that you want to use for the app or website.
  iii. Click on "Hide my email" if you want your email address to remain private. Apple generates a random and unique email address that will be used to forward email

from the app or website to your real email address.

Sign in to an app or website account

- On your Mac, click the Sign In With Apple or Continue With Apple button.

- Enter your login password on your Mac (you may need to enter your Apple ID password instead) or use Touch ID to sign in if your Mac supports Touch ID.

You can also sign in from another device (iPhone, iPad, Apple Watch, or Apple TV) that you're signed in to with the same Apple ID.

Modify the address used to deliver email from websitesand apps

If you hidden your email address when you created an account and you have multiple email addresses associated with your Apple ID in Apple ID settings, you can change the address to which emails are forwarded.

- Choose "Apple" on Mac > "System Preferences" and touch "Apple ID".

- Click in the sidebar on "Name, Phone, E-Mail" and then next to "Hide my e-mail" on "Edit".
- Select a different email address and click "Done".

Changing Sign In with Apple settings for a websiteor an app

- Choose "Apple" on Mac > "System Preferences" and touch "Apple ID".
- Click in the sidebar on "Password & Security" and then next to "Apps using your Apple ID" on "Edit".
- Click an app or website in the sidebar, and do any of the following:

i. Deactivate e-mail forwarding: Click on "Switch off". You will then no longer receive any further emails from the app or website.

ii. Stop using Sign in with Apple: Click Stop Using Apple ID. The next time you sign in to the app or website, you may be asked to create a new account.

SET UP SECURITY FOR YOUR MAC

There are several ways you can make your Mac more secure.

Use strong passwords

To protect your Mac computer and the data and information on it, you should use passwords and choose your passwords so that they are not easy to guess.

Force user to log in

If other people have access to your Mac, you should set up each person using the Mac as a separate user, requiring each of those users to log in. This will prevent unauthorized people from using the Mac. In addition, the individual user files are strictly separated and users only have access to their own personal files and settings. Users cannot see or change other users' files or settings.

Protect Mac when not in use

You can set up your Mac to log the current user out if there is no activity on the Mac for a period of time. For more information, see Logging out of your Mac when inactive . You should also ensure that a password must be entered in order to wake up from hibernation or screensaver. You also have the option to define an active corner that you can click to instantly lock your screen.

Limit the number of administrative users

For a Mac, one or more people can be defined as users with administrator rights . By default, the user who carries out the initial configuration of the Mac is entered as the administrator.

Administrators have the right; create other users; manage and delete, install and remove software,and change settings. For these reasons, an administrator should create a standard user account and use it when administrator rights are not required. If the security of a standard user's account is threatened, the potential harm is far less than if an administrator's account is threatened. If more than one person uses your Mac, keep the number of users with administrative privileges to a minimum.

Encrypting data on Mac utilizing theFile Vault

You can use File Vault encryption to protect personal or confidential data and information on your Mac from being viewed or copied by unauthorized persons. File Vault encodes the data stored on a Mac so that it is protected and can only be read if the correct login password is entered.

MANAGE PASSWORDS WITH KEYCHAINS ON MAC

Your passwords, account numbers and other confidential information that you use on your Mac computers and iOS and iPad devices every day can be tracked and protected with the macOS keychains.

The Keychain Access app on your Mac allows you to view and manage your keyrings. By using iCloud Keychain, you can keep your passwords and other sensitive information up-to-date on all of your devices.

What a key chain is

A keyring is an encoded or encrypted container for securestorage of your account names and passwords for yourwebsites,servers,apps and Mac, as well as card numbers or bank account PINs.

When you visit a website or an email account, it is possible you to save the password on your keyring. This has the advantage that you don't have to remember the password or enter it every time.

Every Mac user has a login keychain. Your login keychain password is the same as the password you use to log in to your Mac. If your login password is reset on your Mac by an administrator, you'll also need to reset your login keychain password.

Keychain management

The "Keychain Management" app on your Mac enables you to view and manage your log-in and other keyrings and thus also the objects that are reliably saved in your keyrings. This includes, for example, keys, certificates, passwords, account information and notes. If you have forgotten a password, you can find it in the keychain.

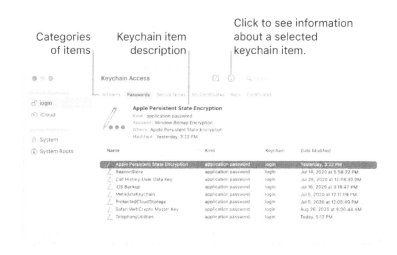

iCloud keychain

your iCloud Keychain can be used to storecredit card and the website credentials you use with Auto-

Complete in Safari, and your Wi-Fi data, If you use cloud. Your iCloud keyring automatically keeps this information up to date on all your Mac computers and iOS and iPadOS devices. The iCloud keyring also stores login data for the accounts that you use in Mail, Contacts, Calendar and Messages, so that these credentials are available on all of your devices.

ATTENTION: If you use passwords and credit cards online, you can have Safari save them in your keyring and fill them out for you automatically. If iCloud Keychain is used on Mac and your iPadOSandiOS devices, Safari can restore the saved data on any device.

RESET MAC LOGIN PASSWORD

It may be necessary to reset the login password (for example, if you have forgotten your password and no help is available to remember your password).

When a user's password is reset, a new default keyring is created in which the user's passwords are saved.

Reset login password using Apple ID

If you 've linked your user account to your Apple ID , you can use your Apple ID to reset your login password.

- Choose "Apple" on Mac > "Restart" or press the on / off switch of the computer and tap "Restart".
- Click on your user account and on the question mark in the password field. Then touch the button ⊙next to " Reset it with your Apple ID".
- Enter an Apple ID and password and click "Next".

Heed the instructions to reset your sign in password.

Reset login password using a recovery key

Once you've turned on FileVault encryption and created a recovery key, you can use the recovery key to reset your login password.

- Choose "Apple" on Mac > "Restart" or press the on / off button of the computer and tap "Restart".
- Click on your user account and on the question mark in the password field. Then touch the this

205

button next to " Reset it with your recovery key".

- Write the recovery key and tap "Next".

Adhere to the direction to reset your sign in password.

Reset another user's password

An administrator can reset other users' passwords.

- on Mac, Choose "Apple" > "System Settings" and tap "Users & Groups".

  When the lock is closed in the lower left, click the lock to unlock System Preferences.

- Choose a user and touch "Reset password".

IMPORTANT INFORMATION ABOUT THE SECURITY OF YOUR MAC

Attention: negligence on your part to follow these safety guidelines could result in fire, electric shock, or other injury, or damage to your MacBook Pro or other property.

Integrated battery. Do not attempt to replace or remove the battery yourself as this can damage the battery, which in turn can lead to overheating and personal injury. The built-in lithium-ion battery may only be replaced by Apple or an authorized service partner and must be recycled or disposed of separately from household waste. Always dispose of used batteries in accordance with the applicable environmental guidelines. Do not expose your MacBook Pro to extreme heat sources, such as radiant heaters or open fires, which can reach temperatures in excess of 100 ° C.

Handling. Handle your MacBook Pro carefully. The device is made of metal, glass and plastic and contains sensitive electronic components. Lay the MacBook Pro on a safe work surface that permitenough airflow beneath and around the computer. MacBook Pro can be damaged if dropped, punctured, broken, or exposed to an open flame, liquids, oils, and solutions. Do not use the MacBook Pro if it is damaged - for example, the screen is cracked - as there is a risk of personal injury.

Contact with liquids. Do not use your MacBook Pro near sources of moisture such as beverages, oils, solutions, sinks, bathtubs and shower trays, etc. Protect your MacBook Pro from moisture, moisture or rain, snow or fog.

To charge the battery. Charge the MacBook Pro only with the 61W or 96W USB-C power adapter and USB-C charging cable provided, or with a third-party cable and power adapter that is compatible with USB-C and complies with international and regional guidelines and safety standards . Other power adapters may not meet applicable safety standards, and charging with such power adapters can cause life-threatening injury.

Using a damaged power adapter or cord, or charging in a damp environment could result in a fire, electric shock, or other injury, or damage to your MacBook Pro or other property. If you're using the included 61W or 96W USB-C power adapter and USB-C charging cable to charge your MacBook Pro, make sure the USB-C charging cable is properly connected to the power adapter before connecting the power adapter to the Connect power grid

Long exposure to heat. Your MacBook Pro and the 61W or 96W power adapter may become very warm with normal use. The MacBook Pro and the 61W Power Adapter or 96W Power Adapter meet the required limit values for surface temperatures, which are defined in national and international safety standards. It should be noted, however, that prolonged contact with a heated surface can be uncomfortable or cause burns, even in the permissible temperature range.

To curtail overheating make sure that there is sufficient airflow around the MacBook Pro or 96W or61W power adapter and wield it properly. Use common sense and avoid situations where your skin will come into contact with a device or power adapter if it has been on or connected to a power source for a long time. For instance, do not position a device or power adapter under your body while being plugged into an electrical outlet. Do not place the device or power adapter under a blanket, pillow, or your body when the device or power adapter is connected to the mains. Never insert objects into the ventilation slots. Doing so can be dangerous and cause your computer to overheat. Never place objects on the keyboard while your MacBook Pro is in use. If you're using your MacBook Pro with it on your thighs and the device is giving off too much heat, place it on a sturdy, smooth surface with adequate ventilation. Be especially careful if your body is so disposed that it does not react immediately to high temperatures and heat.

Hearing loss. Listening to music and other audio media at high volumes can damage your hearing. Background noise as well as continuous playback at high volumes can result in sounds being perceived as being quieter than they actually are. Use only compatible earbuds, headphones, or earplugs with your MacBook Pro. Turn on the audio and check the volume before inserting the earbuds in your ears or putting on headphones.

CAUTION: To avoid hearing damage, the volume should not be set too high and the device should only be used for a limited period at very high volume.

Repair. Your MacBook Pro does not contain any user-serviceable parts. Under no circumstances should you attempt to open, disassemble, or repair your MacBook Pro, or replace any components. Disassembling the MacBook Pro can damage the device and cause personal injury. If your MacBook Pro is damaged, not working properly, or has been exposed to liquids, contact Apple or an Apple Authorized Service Center, such as an Apple Authorized Service Provider. You risk damaging your computer by trying to open your MacBook Pro. Such damage is not covered by the MacBook Pro warranty.

Navigation. Maps, driving directions, and location-based apps depend on data services. These data services are subject to change and may not be available in certain countries or areas. As a result, certain maps, driving directions, or location-based information may not be available, accurate, or complete. Compare the provided, location-based information with your surroundings and, if in doubt, take into account any signs that are available. Do not use such services during activities that require your full attention. Always observe billboards and signs, as well as existing laws and regulations, when using the navigation system, and always act with appropriate attention and common sense.

Exposure to radio frequencies. The MacBook Pro uses radio signals to connect to wireless networks.

Interference with medical equipment. The MacBook Pro contains components that emit electromagnetic radiation (including magnets) that can impair pacemakers, defibrillators, and other medical devices and apparatus. Keep your medical device away from your MacBook Pro. Consult your doctor or device manufacturer for more detailed information about your medical device. If there are warning signs MacBook Pro is infringingon your pacemaker or another medical device, desist from using the MacBook Pro.

Physical complaints. Talk to your doctor and temporarily stop using the MacBook Pro if you experience other physical symptoms (such as seizures, fainting, or eye or headaches) that you think may be caused by using the MacBook Pro.

Repetitive motion sequences. With repetitive motion sequences (for example when capturing texts for a long time or playing games on the MacBook Pro for a long time), complaints can occasionally occur in the hands, arms, shoulders, neck area and other parts of the body. If you experience these symptoms, stop using your MacBook Pro and talk to your doctor.

Choking hazard. Certain MacBook Pro accessories can present a suffocation hazard to infants and young children. Keep these accessories away from infants and young children.

Activities with far-reaching consequences. MacBook Pro should not be used in an area where malfunction could result in death, personal injury, or serious environmental damage.

Explosive and other atmospheric conditions. Do not charge the MacBook Pro in areas with a potentially explosive atmosphere (such as gas stations) or in areas where the air contains a high concentration of flammable chemicals. Exposing the MacBook Pro to high concentrations of industrial chemicals, such as evaporating liquefied gas such as helium, can damage the MacBook Pro or affect its functionality. Follow all notice boards, warnings, and instructions.